The Autonomy
of Religious Belief

UNIVERSITY OF NOTRE DÀME STUDIES IN THE PHILOSOPHY OF RELIGION

Number 2

The Autonomy of Religious Belief

A Critical Inquiry

Edited with an Introduction by
FREDERICK J. CROSSON

UNIVERSITY OF NOTRE DAME PRESS
NOTRE DAME   LONDON

Library of Congress Cataloging in Publication Data

Main entry under title:

The Autonomy of religious belief.

   (Notre Dame studies on the philosophy of
religion ; v. 2)
   1. Religion and language — Addresses, essays,
lectures.   2. Religion — Philosophy — Addresses,
essays, lectures.   I. Crosson, Frederick James,
1926–   II. Series.
BL65.L2A95   200'.1   81–50461
ISBN 0–268–00596–6   AACR2

Manufactured in the United States of America

Contents

Contributors

J. M. CAMERON is Emeritus Professor of Philosophy at St. Michael's College, University of Toronto. Among his books are his Terry Lectures, *Images of Authority* and *On the Idea of a University.*

LOUIS MACKEY is Professor of Philosophy at the University of Texas, Austin. He is the author of *Kierkegaard: A Kind of Poet.*

D. Z. PHILLIPS is Professor of Philosophy at the University of Swansea in Wales. He has published numerous works in the philosophy of religion, including *The Concept of Prayer* and *Religion Without Explanation.*

KAI NIELSEN is Professor of Philosophy at the University of Calgary. His related works are *Contemporary Critiques of Religion* and *Ethics Without God.*

KENNETH SAYRE is Professor of Philosophy at the University of Notre Dame. He has written extensively about cybernetics and the implications of information theory and also about Plato. His latest books are *Cybernetics and the Philosophy of Mind* and *Plato's Analytic Method.*

WILLIAM P. ALSTON is Professor of Philosophy at Syracuse University. He has published *Philosophy of Language* and *Religious Belief and Philosophical Thought.*

Introduction

These essays address the question of whether religion can be adequately understood as a "form of life," taking the latter phrase in the sense of Ludwig Wittgenstein. It is fair to say that their collective conclusion is that the answer is no—although the qualifications on and the reasons for that answer of course differ from one author to another.

Wittgenstein used the notion of a form of life to exhibit the fact that knowing a language is not simply acquiring a vocabulary and rules of grammar, but rather "to imagine a language is to imagine a form of life." Language is an organic part of the way of life of a human group. The meaning of utterances is interwoven with the actions of that way of life; the meaning is not a timeless idea in the mind of speaker and hearer, identical for all men everywhere.

Herder, two centuries before, had set the historical specificity of cultures against the Enlightenment's universal norms of rationality by insisting on the indistinguishable link between language and thought. Rejecting the notion of an identical human nature, he argued that different languages entail different standards of rationality and value.

Wittgenstein's notion, however, is not tied so tightly to the concept of a *Volk* and a culture. For him, the notion of a "language-game" introduces an internal heterogeneity into the language of a people. Thus the scientific language-game has its rules of what can be meaningfully said, but those rules have no legitimate claim to hegemony over other language-games. Moral discourse

1

(e.g., commanding, promising, commending) and religious discourse, among others, have their own meaningfulness, as does every distinctive language-game. (What distinguishes a specific language-game remains ambiguous.)

Alston expresses this claim by saying that a distinct language-game has "epistemic autonomy": its statements are justified, not by appeal to some more fundamental or objective discourse (scientific, say, or observational), but by reference to paradigm-cases in which the use of such statements has been learned.

On the basis of Wittgenstein's analyses, some philosophers and theologians were led (not without some ground in passing remarks of his) to claim not only that religious discourse constituted such a language-game, but that this meant that such discourse was immune from any criticism which assessed it by allegedly universal but actually alien standards of meaning and truth. D. Z. Phillips in his essay calls this position "internalism" and finds it untenable, at least without serious qualification.

For even if one admits the correctness of Wittgenstein's analysis (and succeeds in stifling the tendency to believe that there still must be some overarching criterion of meaning and truth which relates all the others), the heterogeneity of language-games within a culture where the cake of custom has been broken entails a tangled crisscrossing and interpenetration of terms. Words get picked up from one context and modified by their use in another, borrowed back, extended, pruned. In this process, no language-game can stand apart.

Each of the essays touches on the consequences of this situation and assesses the import for religious belief.

J. M. Cameron proposes to test the notion of a form of life as providing a comprehensive mode of understanding of religion by taking Christendom as an example. He argues that the associated notions of a form of life and a language-game have successfully exorcised certain philosophical bewitchments of our understanding. But their application to religion does not yield such definitive fruits.

He considers two examples which illustrate the limitations of such an understanding of religion. The first is that of transitions within Christendom from one form of life to another, which makes clear that Christendom is a complex cluster of forms of life, overlapping and interpenetrating in multifarious ways the political, cultural, historical dimensions of Western civilization as a whole. It does not stand by itself as a homogeneous and integral form of life.

The second example, Kierkegaard's *Attack Upon "Christendom,"* shows that the notion is also potentially heteronomous internally, in the dimension of depth. Critical reflection on the religious form of life of Danish Lutheranism is possible from within, from a deeper stratum of comprehension of the Christian kerygma. This deeper point of vantage not only shows the possibility of auto-criticism and (again) of subterranean connections with other depths (Socrates) but raises the question of whether a manifest religious form of life such as the functioning Danish Church might not be recognized to be, in validly warranted judgment, moribund, however alive it may appear.

The result is that the usefulness of understanding religion as a form of life is undeniable but limited. Cameron's conclusion argues that this is not, in fact, contrary to Wittgenstein's fundamental philosophical aim, which was to move toward an *Übersicht*, a synoptic understanding of language.

Louis Mackey's gracefully written discourse takes Bonaventure as an exemplar of the way in which revelation, as the disclosure of an Other who confronts us beyond any expectancy and beyond capture in language, subverts the form of life which is our everyday language. One may attempt to view the Christian kerygma as a revised language-game, but to do so is to miss the way in which it overturns the relation of myth to philosophy by bringing to the commonsense world of Aristotelian things a signification which undermines the very notions of truth and reality in the familiar world.

For the first substances which anchor the predicates of Aristotelian discourse are revealed to be *ex alio*, to be most truly in God, *esse in aeterna ratione*. The world is a text to be read, not a collection of things to be sorted and related. It is sacred scripture and not philosophy which reveals and conceals the meaning of the world. Hence, Christianity is not a form of life but a deformation of language and of any life formed by immanent standards of intelligibility.

D. Z. Phillips identifies part of the effect of Wittgenstein's linking of a language to a form of life as a critique of 'externalism', i.e., the assumption that there is one standard of meaning for every language-game. Wittgenstein showed that the meaning of utterances must be understood by reference to the language-game of which they are a part, and this in turn by reference to the form of life in which it is embedded. This led some to think of the various aspects of human life as heterogeneous, semantically independent, at least from any general criterion of meaning, a position which Phillips terms "internalism."

But opposition to externalism need not imply internalism, if the latter is understood to deny *any* kind of connection between one *Lebensform*, e.g., religious belief, and other aspects of life. Phillips distinguishes several such pictures of internalism which are not tenable. One is religious individualism, which postulates a direct relationship between the believer and God, independent of any social or cultural changes. But there is no hiding place in the heart immune from culture and change, no "bare Christianity" untouched by history. A second is religious rationalism, the position that formal arguments secure the validity of religious belief, no matter how the map of learning shifts. Phillips denies the possibility of such time-independent proofs, asserting that they live from faith rather than the reverse. A third picture is religious accommodation: Christianity can adapt to cultural change without substantial transformation by shifting to new forms and formulas. But whether such a transformation can come about is not a matter of intention for the church: perhaps it will be able to speak with authority under new forms, but that cannot be foreseen. Christianity may not perdure, historically.

Does this mean that religious truths cannot be eternal? If to be such they must be immune from all contingencies, then—yes. But there is conceptual confusion here, for the "eternity" of geometry is not the eternity of which religion speaks.

Kai Nielsen, after sketching his understanding of Wittgenstein's position on religious discourse as a language-game, insists that the question of what God is, and whether he is, is not a deviant question. Even if one concedes Wittgenstein's arguments about the nonempirical but certain character of framework-propositions, the issue of securing reference for the term 'God' remains a legitimate one. That assertions such as "God is real" are not questioned in the religious language-game doesn't entail that they are not questionable. And the query "Is God real?" is not deviant in the same way as "do physical objects exist?" or "did the past exist?" since even believers can find the query meaningful.

Kenneth Sayre criticizes two common conceptions of religion and proposes instead what he calls a perceptual model of belief in God. Against an intentional notion of religious belief, namely as a mental attitude toward that entity called 'God', he notes that this notion requires a correct description of the entity as grasped in the mental attitude. The contradictions in this regard among various religions as well as among philosophers indicate the problems in using this notion to decide whether someone believes in God. Against the notion that religion consists in following certain practices, he observes that not only does it not allow any means of distinguishing between true and false beliefs, but it cannot admit ordinary statements about someone coming to accept the practices of a given religion because of what he believes.

He proposes instead to construe belief in God as a certain manner of perceiving the world, following in this proposal some hints in Wittgenstein's notebooks. He develops this proposal by means of examples which illustrate a disposition to perceive the world as having a comprehensive significance.

William Alston, in order to address the question of whether Christian discourse is a distinct language-game, finds it necessary first to sharpen the notion of a "language-game," for Wittgenstein uses the term of a number of things without suggesting any single criterion of individuation. Alston argues that a distinct language-game differs from others ontologically (it deals with categoreally distinct things), conceptually (distinctive categoreal characteristics and applicable concepts), and epistemologically (the justification of its assertions is not derived or inferred from another language-game but learned in using it). It therefore has epistemic autonomy, but he denies that it has ontological autonomy: it does not have distinctive concepts of truth and reality.

Christian discourse, he maintains, meets these criteria in asserting the categoreal uniqueness of God and hence his conceptual distinctiveness, and by grounding the epistemic justification of its assertions in the practice of Christian life.

He considers a number of objections to this thesis (not played by all, alternative religious language-games, uncertainty of "moves," etc.) and responds by asserting that different orders of reality imply differential modes of cognitive access to the real, as well as by noting that something more than potential accessibility is necessary, namely faith, a not-purely-cognitive attitude of the individual.

It is clear, even from this brief summary, that none of the authors defends a radical autonomy for the language-game of religious discourse. But if "internalism" is untenable, Phillips is right to assert that that does not mean that "externalism" is tenable. If the notion of religion as a form of life seems not as philosophically consequential as some have thought, that is because exploring that notion has helped to clarify both what a form of life is and what religion is.

The Idea of Christendom

J. M. CAMERON

Unwary and inexperienced theologians seem to acquire a disposition to cast themselves with rapacity onto
the dimly visible bodies of misunderstood theories. The
Big Bang theory of the origin of the universe is supposed
to vindicate the dogmatically certain principle of *creatio ex
nihilo*, just as two generations ago Heisenberg's Uncertainty Principle was thought to do a similar service for the
idea of free will. There seems to have grown up a
disposition among the desperate to profit from Wittgenstein's notion of *Lebensform*, 'form of life'. It seems to be
thought that we have here a device for rendering the
various claims made by religious believers invulnerable
to criticism: scientific, historical, moral or what have you.
The dogma of Transubstantiation or the doctrine of
Karma gets its sense from the role of its linguistic expressions in the form of life, liturgical or other, of the
believing community. One who stands outside the believing community stands outside the expression in question.

Professor Antony Flew and I were once seated side by
side at a meeting of philosophers addressed by a well-
known philosopher of religion, later to be elevated to the
episcopal chair of the great Joseph Butler. He set forward the remarkable statement: "The resurrection narratives are logically odd"; and under the pressure of the
discussion, it became clear that he meant, among other
things, that one couldn't raise in connection with them

the crude question: Are they true or false? For once Professor Flew and I were forced into total agreement with each other. If such stratagems are to be permitted, it will turn out that believers will be told they don't mean what, historically, they have certainly meant when talking about, e.g., the resurrection of Jesus Christ; and unbelievers will be told to keep off the grass and talk to themselves in their own territory. To protect the resurrection narratives from historical criticism by labeling them "logically odd" belongs, or so it seems to me, to the same family of devices as the use of the idea of 'form of life' for defensive or apologetic purposes. (I ought to add that the "unwary and inexperienced" I have in mind commonly *are* theologians, not philosophers.)

The idea of 'language-game' and the idea of 'form of life' are intimately connected, just because a language-game consists of "language and actions into which it is woven."[1] And "to imagine a language means to *imagine* a form of life";[2] and not only is to *imagine* a language to imagine a form of life, "the *speaking* of a language is [also] part of an activity, or of a form of life."[3] Language and actions are interwoven; this is why we have to think of language not as something which occurs *within* a given form of life but as an organic part, as it were, of the total natural history of a human group. "Commanding, questioning, recounting, chatting, are as much a part of our natural history as walking, eating, drinking, playing."[4]

We can take all such statements as enormous platitudes—"Who deniges of it, Betsy?"—if we come across them in isolation, as though they were the *obiter dicta* of some relaxed and whiffling social anthropologist. Of course, they get their point from the philosophical problems they are designed to resolve or dissolve. We have also to remember that it is a Wittgensteinian principle that philosophy only states what everyone admits (or perhaps better, can be brought to admit, for this emphasizes the Socrates-and-the-slave-boy situation that is, or so he hopes, the situation of the teacher of philosophy faced with his pupils). These problems are those of the mingled Cartesian and empiricist traditions in Europe: roughly, the family of problems generated by the Cartesian principle that the mind is better known than the body (Second Meditation). Perhaps the most familiar example of this is Locke's view of how words get their meaning; they are "articulate sounds" used as "signs of internal conceptions" and made to "stand as marks for the ideas within [a man's] own mind, whereby they might be made known to others, and the thoughts of men's minds be conveyed from one to another."[5] Wittgenstein's account shows that if this were right, no one could ever learn a language, and the use of the linked ideas of language-game and form of life successfully disposes of the Cartesian-empiricist example of the bewitchment of the intelligence by means of language.

I think that in this matter Wittgenstein's arguments are satisfactory and that the dilemmas or predicaments generated by the Cartesian premise have been robbed of the interest they used to have. This doesn't mean that we are dispensed from repeating our philosophical history; although historically this cluster of problems comes from Descartes, it seems evident that such dilemmas or predicaments were known to the Greeks, and I dare say to the Chinese. This seems to be what Wittgenstein is getting at when he remarks that "the problems arising through a misinterpretation of our forms of language have the character of *depth*. They are deep disquietudes; their roots are as deep in us as the forms of our language and their significance is as great as the importance of our language."[6] A disquietude so deep, a puzzlement that ranges over long periods of history and many different civilizations, this is for him what marks out the field of philosophical interest. If it is possible, as it is, for those equipped with the linguistic forms of Chinese to puzzle over the paradoxes of material implication, if the Greeks of the fifth century B.C. could find difficulty in seeing just how the concept of truth applies to moral statements, then it is unlikely that brisk refutations of particular epistemological theories, even those refutations that are soup boiled down from the bones of the Wittgensteinian corpus, will free us from our disposition to set ourselves philosophical problems of a kind that may turn out on investigation to be both bewitchments of the intelligence, through a failure to know whither our misunderstanding of our language is taking us, and also variations upon old themes.

I conclude, then, that there is nothing restrictive about the concept language-game/form of life, nothing, at least at first glance, that makes it impossible for Europeans and North Americans of some degree of education to grasp the meanings of individual expressions or whole sublanguages that are in the first place remote from their own experience or from their own linguistic metropolis or suburb. I am encouraged to think this by the cautionary remarks, as I take them to be, of Wittgenstein himself. In the middle of his early discussion of language-games of an elementary kind, he notes that some may have a difficulty over the simplicity of his examples and may argue that such invented languages are useless as heuristic examples since they are essentially incomplete.

> If you want to say that this [the invented languages *supra* consisted only of orders] shews them to be incomplete, ask yourself whether our language is complete; — whether it was so before the symbolism of chemistry and the notation of the infinitesimal calculus were incorporated in it; for these are, so to speak, suburbs of our language. (And how many houses or streets does it take before a town begins to be a town?) Our language can be seen as an ancient city; a maze of little streets and squares, of old and new houses, and of houses with additions from various periods; and this surrounded by a multitude of new boroughs with straight regular streets and uniform houses.[7]

I find this image full of reverberations, at least one of them provoked with intention. We are bound to think of the solemn repudiation of the ancient city, with its maze of little streets gathered round cathedral and palace, in the second part of the *Discourse on Method*. It seems possible that Wittgenstein had this passage in mind:

> those ancient cities which were originally mere boroughs, and have become large towns in process of time, are as a rule badly laid out, as compared with those towns of regular pattern that are laid out by a designer on an open plain to suit his fancy; while the buildings severally considered are often equal or superior artistically to those in planned towns, yet, in view of their arrangement—here a large one, there a small—and the way they make the streets twisted and irregular, one would say that it was chance that placed them so, not the will of men who had the use of reason.[8]

Here the unplanned city is an image of what is received from tradition, with all its irregularities, patchings, discordant themes, all that irritates and frustrates one for whom mathematics is the only science God has so far bestowed upon men. Wittgenstein is saying, as it were, that this is where we live, in the many-layered, labyrinthine city of human culture, and that there is something hopelessly wrong about the ambition to make the clean start, to found the geometrical city where all is clear at a glance, leaving behind us the ruins of the past.

I

I propose to take the idea of Christendom as a case for asking where a consideration of *Lebensform* will take us. Much of what I say will consist of observations on what Wittgenstein calls the natural history of men, and although this is not in itself what Wittgenstein or anyone else calls philosophy, it becomes philosophical if it is directed towards the solution or dissolution or even, simply, the more perspicuous rendering of those problems that won't go away when we try to handle them in accordance with ordinary critical methods.

'Christendom' I shall understand as designating a state of affairs in human history that begins in the West with Augustine, in the East of course earlier with the transfer of the Empire to Byzantium, and persists down to our own day and perhaps well into the future. It is to be identified in the main with particular spaces that contract and expand from time to time; there are what one might call fully realized expansions, as to the Americas in the sixteenth and seventeenth centuries, or frustrated expansions, as to China, Japan, and India in the seventeenth century; and there are the contractions, as in North Africa and the eastern Mediterranean. From the past Christendom has absorbed philosophies, literatures, sciences, political models, and so on, most immediately from the Hellenistic world; but it seems hard to place any limit to the openness of this particular fragment of human history to the past. It seems likely that our political forms, our moral maxims, our jurisprudential ideas, not to speak of the archaic forms that, it seems, have some role in shaping how we take our physical world — day and night, sun and moon, water and fire, cold and warmth, sexual and paternal, maternal, and filial relations — are related to strata of the common past now irrecoverable, at least in any straightforward sense. It may shake the mind to notice that Neanderthal men, with whom we may have no direct biological connection, had ceremonials for the burying of the dead.

You will have noticed that I speak of *our* political forms, moral maxims, and so on: I do this to bring out that I am using the term 'Christendom' in such a way that anyone with a Western education lives within it and can't help doing so, in virtue of the legal norms, the literary fictions, the political ideas, the ways of living in

community, et cetera that compel us, if I may adapt
Wittgenstein, "to travel over a wide field of thought criss-
cross in every direction."[9] That is, 'Christendom' is a
complex of forms of life; how we live and move within
this complex will illustrate the usefulness and the frailty
of *Lebensform* as an explanatory device.

I take as my first example of a response to a part of this
complex, one that is well known to literary critics. It is the
violent moment in *Middlemarch* when the heroine, the
natural flow of feeling blocked by her impossible marriage to the aged pseudoscholar Casaubon, receives the
attack of the Roman scene like a wound or a disease:

> after the brief narrow experience of her girlhood she
> was beholding Rome, the city of visible history, where
> the past of a whole hemisphere seems moving in
> funeral procession with strange ancestral images and
> trophies gathered from afar. . . .
>
> To those who have looked at Rome with the quicken-
> ing power of a knowledge which breathes a growing
> soul into all historic shapes, and traces out the sup-
> pressed transitions which unite all contrasts, Rome
> may still be the spiritual centre of the world. But let
> them conceive one more historical contrast: the gigan-
> tic broken revelations of that Imperial and Papal city
> thrust abruptly on the notions of a girl who had been
> brought up in English and Swiss Puritanism, fed on
> meagre Protestant histories and on art chiefly of the
> handscreen sort. . . . The weight of unintelligible
> Rome might lie easily on bright nymphs to whom it
> formed a background for the brilliant picnic of
> Anglo-foreign society; but Dorothea had no such de-
> fence against deep impressions. Ruins and basilicas,
> palaces and colossi, set in the midst of a sordid present,
> where all that was living and warm-blooded seemed
> sunk in the deep degeneracy of a superstition divorced
> from reverence; the dimmer but yet eager Titanic life
> gazing and struggling on walls and ceilings; the long

vistas of white forms whose marble eyes seemed to hold the monotonous light of an alien world; all this . . . at first jarred her as with an electric shock, and then urged themselves on her with that ache belonging to a glut of confused ideas which check the flow of emotion. Forms both pale and glowing took possession of her young sense, and fixed themselves in her memory even when she was not thinking of them, preparing strange associations which remained through her after-years . . . in certain states of dull forlornness Dorothea all her life continued to see the vastness of St. Peter's, the huge bronze canopy, the excited intention in the attitudes and garments of the prophets and evangelists in the mosaics above, and the red drapery which was being hung for Christmas spreading itself everywhere like a disease of the retina.[10]

I called this a violent moment because the Roman scene is received as though the soul were wounded or made sick, stricken or infected. This is a suitable image for a certain kind of induction into a way of life; the wound comes from an unwillingness, one that is all the same without interdictory force, to be brought within a form of life; the sickness, as it were a fever, of the soul comes from the wound, ever open, never quite healed. This half-entry into a form of life takes its quality from the actual situation of Dorothea with all its perplexities of thought and feeling, and here she is a more humanly representative figure than the cool observer, the one who looks in and stays outside. She is contrasted, in the suppressed hysteria of her disturbed Puritanical maidenhood, with one for whom "Rome may still be the spiritual centre of the world"—no doubt Eliot has such a one as Newman in mind; yet although she bears "the weight of *unintelligible* Rome," the impression is deep, the effect for life. It is not as though in Rome she is faced with the otherness of Aztec temples or neolithic fortifications, mere memorials of a dead form of life; her half-entry into Rome is prepared by her education, meagre though it may have been, so that the "Titanic life gazing and struggling on walls and ceilings," the "forms both pale and glowing," take possession of her, she recognizes the prophets and evangelists in the mosaics because she already has some notion of what a prophet or an evangelist is, and this is why "the excited intention" in their attitudes and garments disturbs her: it is as though they had become for her threatening realities, no longer shut up in the sacred volume, but released and hungry, with designs upon Dorothea.

Finally, the strange intimacy of the experience is represented by the magnificent image with which the passage ends: "like a disease of the retina." It is not that Dorothea is the victim of tricks of perceptive, optical illusion; such deceptions leave the one who sees aloof, uninvolved; she received Rome into the privileged organs of perception, onto the surface of the eyes, signs of the soul that get their life (in this passage) from the implied contrast with the dead marble eyes that represent the level light of pagan antiquity. It wouldn't be right to say that Rome is a complete enigma to Dorothea: an enigma doesn't trouble us in quite this sharp way. She hasn't come "into a strange country with entirely strange traditions" in which " we do not *understand* the people."[11] The effect is rather that of a dream in which a road or a room is strange and yet familiar, disturbing just because it is not simply a foreign fact. Dorothea in Rome thus may stand for one way in which we move within the complex of Christendom.

I observe in connection with this example that, trembling upon the frontier of two forms of life—one thoroughly experienced and grounded in habit, the other vaguely apprehended through visible signs that have some compelling power only because Dorothea's education provides a narrow but sufficient, if barely sufficient, ground for new apprehensions—she is filled with passion and desire, strong impulses to flee away and at the same time go forward into the not yet embraced. The images of pain and sickness bring out how wrenching and debilitating an experience it is to pass from one culture to another. Nevertheless, the "pale and glowing" forms *take possession of her*, and this is seduction rather than rape; there is that in Dorothea which reaches out with a disguised appetite for the dread forms and their half-divined intentions. The whole experience reflects a torn consciousness; the vehemence of the response seems to transcend the occasion. If we ask why this should be so, then I think one answer is that Dorothea, this "girl . . . brought up in English and Swiss Puritanism," trembles on the edge of what she takes to be absolute prohibitions. Like all human beings she has within her "a terrible, fierce, and lawless class of desires," desires that in decent people are only satisfied in dreams, in which the soul "is ready for any deed of blood, and there is no unhallowed food it will not eat"[12] (we have already noted the dreamlike quality of the experience). The charm of the mixture of paganism and Catholicism, which to her Protestant sensibility is the spectacle of Rome, is that it represents the gratification of what has been deeply repressed but has now been released in fantasy by her dim awareness of her frontier situation; but the experience is also threatening in its invitation to Dorothea to throw off the absolute prohibitions of her Protestant formation.

Well-educated people tend toward antinomianism, and it is important that Dorothea is narrowly and imperfectly educated. If she were more sophisticated the spectacle of Rome might still make her giddy, but the movement towards a foreign form of life would be more a flirtation, less the solemn violation of a prohibition that adultery is; indeed, the effect of sophistication might be to raise in her questions about any assertion that there are deep qualitative differences between flirtation and adultery. But Dorothea lives at the level of morality, not that of the aesthetic, where all ideas, including deeds of blood and the eating of unhallowed foods, incest and the desecration of tombs, are interesting ideas. Here the Dorotheas have even an epistemological advantage in that they are unlikely to neglect the importance of absolute prohibitions in any viable form of human life.

To pass from one form of life to another, as in conversion, is not simply to change one's point of view — "point of view" is closely linked with taking life at the level of the aesthetic — but to turn the whole of the person concerned around. Take the case of one who did not tremble on the frontier but advanced over it, passing from one form of life to another: Ruth the Moabitess. Naomi says to Ruth: "Behold, thy sister-in-law is gone back unto her people and unto her gods. . . ." And Ruth said, "Intreat me not to leave thee or to return from following after thee: for whither thou goest, I will go; and where thou lodgest, I will lodge: thy people shall be my people, and thy God my God."[13] The utterance that effects the transfer gets its solemnity and force from the change from the gods of the Moabites to the God of Israel, and this is no shift in a speculative point of view but the adoption of a new set of injunctions and prohibitions, though in this case it is not a wrenching experience, for Ruth "clave unto" Naomi.[14]

To be a citizen of the world is to have the capacity to pass from one form of life to another, to move from the city to the suburbs and back again, and thus also to acquire a capacity to imagine a diversity of forms of life; but just because the transitions for such a one are relatively painless, there is a tendency to fail to grasp the weight and seriousness for a given way of life of the set of prohibitions and injunctions that give it solidity and persistence through time. We see this in the crassness of aspects of social anthropology before Evans-Pritchard and in the preoccupations with formal connections of the Structuralists. Here Dorothea, trembling on the frontier, and Ruth, knowing the seriousness of abandoning her own gods but doing so happily, with a loving will, are better models, not just as better human beings, but as better, more perceptive appraisers of what is involved in so dreadful a transition.

The situation that faces Dorothea is that of a possible transition within Christendom; she endures the possibility of moving from a suburb into the twisted streets and the darkness of the ancient city. Ruth's transition, from the gods of the Moabites to the God of Israel, is more extreme, indeed, is qualitatively different.

Now, there are many transitions within Christendom, and many ways of facing them. The wanderings of the peoples in modern times, from the old to the new world and, within Europe, from the poorer south and east to the more opulent north-west, provide examples, and from such shifts in forms of life many illuminating accounts have come. The complexity of what has happened since the sixteenth century is so great that no straightforward account is possible. What is striking is the persistence of forms within forms, ways of ordering human life that recur like themes and motifs in musical structures and that, like such themes, are often subtly varied so that we may miss the identity which gathers together the variations. Take, for example, the variations on the theme of the religious life offered by the monks of the desert, those of the Benedictine tradition, and the friars that spring up with the revival of town life in the thirteenth century. And then think of the gathered communities, what Troeltsch calls the "sect-type," Anabaptists and Quakers, that correspond sociologically, for us, to the religious life in medieval and Counter-Reformation Catholicism. To think one's way through such complexities requires a power of imagination and an intellectual tact best exemplified in this century in the work of Max Weber.

One of the most interesting, though it is hard to get the description of it right—perhaps it is enough to refer to it without much description—of the transitions that are, so to speak, available to us, is that in which we pass, often within a single country, from one form of life to another simply by moving a short distance in space. Switzerland offers the most interesting and perhaps the clearest examples. If one passes from the canton of Geneva to that of the Valais, the change is palpable. The pace of life changes, things are different to the ear and the nose, even the sky seems a different sky. Life in the Valais seems relaxed and unbuttoned, tidiness seems no longer a major virtue, the image of the crucified one starts up out of the street and the hedgerow. (An American parallel would be the transition from North to South—I remember this vividly from twenty years ago: the crossing of the state line from Indiana to Kentucky.) These seem slight matters. But it appears likely that it was from the felt difference between the Catholic and the Protestant parts of Germany that the first impulse to write *The Protestant Ethic and the Spirit of Capitalism* came.

II

I want now to speak of another kind of movement or journey, that in which the form of life—strictly, complex of forms—within which a religious man exists is explored at a deeper level within itself. This is almost a mining operation. It involves separating what has been confused, articulating what has not yet been articulated or has been forgotten. It is essentially a matter of *correcting* what is taken to be, by most of those who share the form of life, the sense of what they do and say. On some views this isn't possible; it is not possible, that is, in some accounts of what Professor Kai Nielsen, irresistibly, calls "Wittgensteinian fideism." In some accounts it seems there would be difficulty in incorporating into a description (and philosophers are said to be restricted to describing)[15] any idea of a general misunderstanding, among those who share a form of life, of what it is they are engaged in as actors and speakers. The notion of a general mistake about meaning seems to have no purchase. I suppose we should be able, without abandoning 'fideism', to give an account of a schism. Here the schismatics take off on their own and set up a new if related form of life with a different set of ground rules. We could also recognize that it is a part of the schismatic way of carrying on that they use such concepts as "mistake" and "error" to characterize the procedures—syntax and semantic rules, if you like—of the body they have deserted, though within what language-game the philosopher is making his moves when he offers comparative descriptions of the two forms of life I am not clear.[16]

The exploratory movement I want to look at is that set out in Kierkegaard's polemical writings of 1854–55, translated and collected by Walter Lowrie under the title *Kierkegaard's Attack Upon "Christendom."*[17] Two things ought perhaps to be remembered: that Kierkegaard always insisted that what he wrote, he wrote as a *corrective* (it is hard to remember sometimes that he once wrote that Christianity is the perfection of the truly human); and that he was conscious that he spoke as a dying man, that these were to be his final words.

> I have something on my conscience as a writer [this is written in 1853, before the death of Bishop Mynster]. Let me indicate quite clearly how I feel about it. There is something quite definite I have to say, and I have it so much upon my conscience that (as I feel) I dare not die without having said it. For the moment I die and thus leave this world (as I understand it) I shall in the very same second (at such a speed does it go!), in the very same second I shall be infinitely far away, in a different place where still within the same second (frightful speed!) the question will be put to me: Have you uttered the definite message *quite definitely* . . . ?[18]

What brought Kierkegaard to this point was the death of the worthy and worldly prelate, Bishop Mynster. Professor Martensen, the Court Preacher for the occasion, affirmed in his panegyric on the dead bishop that he was one of the genuine witnesses to the truth and had his place in the "holy chain of witnesses to the truth which stretches through the ages from the days of the Apostles"—"etc.," Kierkegaard adds in derision.[19] Kierkegaard begins quietly by suggesting that this is not even a kindness to Mynster, for "the genuine thing about him was that, as I am firmly convinced, he was willing to admit before God and to himself that by no manner of means was he a witness to the truth."[20] What, then, he asks, is a witness to the truth?

> A witness to the truth is a man who in poverty witnesses to the truth—in poverty, in lowliness, in abasement, and so is unappreciated, hated, abhorred, and then derided, insulted, mocked—his daily bread perhaps he did not always have, so poor was he, but the daily bread of persecution he was richly provided with every day. . . . A witness to the truth, one of the genuine witnesses to the truth, is a man who is scourged, maltreated, dragged from one prison to the other, and then at last—the last promotion, whereby he is admitted to the first class as defined by the Christian protocol, among the genuine witnesses to the truth—then at last—for this is indeed one of those genuine witnesses to the truth of whom Professor Martensen speaks—then at last crucified, or beheaded, or burnt, or roasted on a gridiron, his lifeless body thrown by the executioner in an out-of-the-way place (thus a witness to the truth is buried), or burnt to ashes and cast to the four winds, so that every trace of the "filth" (which the Apostle says *he* was) might be obliterated. . . . and Bishop Mynster, says Professor Martensen, was one of the genuine witnesses to the truth.[21]

This is, Kierkegaard argues, to make a fool of God: "I would rather gamble, carouse, fornicate, steal, murder, than take part in making a fool of God."[22] If I am to twaddle in this way, that is, to say of a worldly prelate that he is a witness or, worse, that the Christian life is for all a pleasant and respectable middle-class existence under an established church and a Christian monarch, then let me "confine myself to talking about this in the parlor, over a cup of tea with my wife and some prating friends, but keep a watch on myself in the pulpit."[23] This kind of thing went on, the rhetoric ever more resourceful, the sarcasm more violent, the irony sharper, until in September 1855 he put down his pen and wrote no more. He died on 11 November 1855, refusing to receive the sacrament "at the hands of the King's officials," that is, the officers of the established church, representatives of Christendom, not of Christianity.

In its particular concerns Kierkegaard's polemic has to do with Denmark as, he believes, an extreme example of a general condition, especially in those Protestant countries—Scandinavia in general, and perhaps a few isolated German states—that are solidly Lutheran, with the alliance of throne and altar in good repair, and other forms of the Christian life unknown, or known only through books and travelers' tales. But his quarrel is in fact with Christendom in general; and with what Christendom had warmed in its bosom—had perhaps conceived—the middle-class democratic revolution of 1848 in which the individual is drowned in the masses, mediocrity overcomes genius and the exceptional, and a mean hedonism prevails in social and domestic life. In such a situation, as distinct from the situation in which the preaching of the Apostles was carried out, the only martyrdom possible—and how Kierkegaard hungered for martyrdom!—was, as he said more than once, that of being trampled to death by geese.

Kierkegaard's attitude to Christendom is by no means entirely negative. In *The Journals* he asks himself why asceticism has entirely disappeared from Protestant cultures, at least in an overt form.

One phase of asceticism . . . may well be considered as over, though not . . . in such a way that subsequent ages do not require to have it inculcated again and again, and in any case, how they stand in need of "grace." But in the history of the human race, or of Christianity, one phase may be looked upon as finished. First of all Christianity had to fight against violent and wild passions and in that respect educate mankind with what in the strictest sense of the word must be called asceticism. The fruit of this education is to have produced a Christian culture and civilisation. . . . this culture and civilisation has at the same time produced a development of rational understanding which is in the process of identifying being a Christian with culture, and with intelligence, desirous of a conceptual understanding of Christianity.

   This is where the struggle must come. . . . It will be a question of establishing the validity of Christianity's incommensurability in this respect, of keeping open the possibility of scandal. . . .[24]

In his final work, then, Kierkegaard splits off the Christian witness from the ordinary physical and institutionalized life of human beings. It has to be said, even if we keep always in mind that what he writes he conceives as "a corrective," that this shows his failure, something one would not have suspected, as a dialectician. It is true that there is something ludicrous about the Danish clergy, royal officials, functioning as ambassadors of the King of Kings; but Kierkegaard forgets that *no* representation of the Divine sovereignty could be other than absurd, even obscene; this is just the kind of problem he spent so much of his life clarifying. He had always a characteristic weakness: it was noted by Theodor Haecker, who said that it was as though Kierkegaard existed as spirit and body, but not as a soul embodied. Hence his repudiation of Regina, for she offered a way—even a way of salvation, religiously speaking—for which he was unfitted, for he knew that the picture of himself as a Christian married man was a false imagination. All the same, he knew what such a life was. He puts a defense of the married state in the mouth of Judge William in *Either/Or*: "The married man . . . has not killed time but has saved it and preserved it in eternity. . . . He solves the great riddle of living in eternity and yet hearing the hall clock strike, and hearing it in such a way that the stroke of the hour does not shorten but prolongs his eternity."[25]

Only through the power of his imagination was he ever able to consider the betrothal to Regina, thinking that he too could solve the great riddle of living in eternity and yet hear the hall clock strike.

Curiously, one who was himself deeply influenced by Kierkegaard and who was even more extreme than Kierkegaard in his turning away from "soulish," embodied life, contrived nevertheless to render for us what is involved in the encounter of human society with absolute spirit and its claims—I mean Kafka. Whereas Kierkegaard, in this final phase in which he tries to split off the Christian witness from ordinary human life, falls into the heresies of the Donatists and Wycliffites, who thought the sacraments were invalid if they came from the hands of the fornicator or the simoniac, Kafka in *The Trial* gives us genuine officers of the Court who are nonetheless mediocre or even malicious men; their relations with women, in particular, are ambiguous; the justice they actually administer they seem not to understand. All the same, we see that they are genuine officers, for they wear their badges, and there is a sense of glory about, behind the door, up the next staircase.

I don't wish to raise the question of how far Kierkegaard was "right" in his attack upon the rootedness of a particular religious culture in Christendom, or, more accurately, upon the identification of a religious culture, that of Christendom, with the religious message set out in the New Testament, that gave it life and form. I think there is a failure on his part to think his position through, even if, still, we bear in mind his being a "corrective." To wish the Church to be the tiny gathered community of the saints has about it a touch of the Manichaean, and this really does express itself in Kierkegaard's misogyny in his last phase, what Lowrie quite correctly calls "the gross disparagement of woman, expressed in terms which in his aesthetical writings he had put in the mouth of the most repulsive characters he created, such as the Ladies' Tailor and the Seducer in 'the Banquet.'" Lowrie adds: "At the bottom of all this was a feeling of horror at the thought of perpetuating a fallen race by sexual reproduction."[26] Lowrie suspects this may have been something he caught from Schopenhauer, whose work he was interested in at this time, but few Christians have needed an excuse to fall momentarily into the Manichaean heresy. (It is extraordinary to find, in our own time, so powerful a mind as that of Simone Weil becoming besotted with Catharism.) Again, he neglects something central in the New Testament, that the *ecclesia* is the great field in which weeds and good grain flourish together, or the great net which holds fish of every kind. The elect are to be "salt" and "light" and "leaven," that is, they exist for the others who, as meat to be cured, or living in darkness, or as the great lump of dough, are not to be despised.

But what is of interest to us is not how far Kierkegaard is just or well balanced or "right," but rather what the possibility of such an operation as that contained in *Attack Upon "Christendom"* has to tell us about the concept "form of life."

First, it brings out certain possibilities within a form of life or a loose and yet recognizably unified complex of forms of life. One of the possibilities is that of auto-criticism. It would be strange to emphasize this were it not for a disposition in us to misread Wittgenstein and think of the meanings established within a form of life as *given*, not only for the philosophical student, but also for the participant in the form. Forms of life are dynamic—

all metaphors that refer to structure (as in the Marxist idea of superstructure) are dangerously misleading here—and our best accounts are betrayals, flat and photographic. The possibility of auto-criticism has to be noted, with all that it implies about innovation, new understandings, recapturings of lost positions; thus we leave ourselves free to go with the flow of life. Then, the example of Kierkegaard, as the example of every major Christian thinker, shows that there are always lines of intellectual communication running to those who on any strict interpretation stand outside the complex to which the thinker belongs. Kierkegaard always felt himself to be metaphysically related to Socrates. His teaching procedure, what he calls "indirect communication," owes as much to the Socrates of Plato as to the New Testament. He may have been a major influence upon Karl Barth, but in this respect, as touching the connection of philosophy with theology, his thought is fundamentally different.

Then, his criticism seems to show the possibility that a form of life may become moribund, even though everything empirical about the form of life remains the same, and that this can be stated *within* the dead form of life. Here is an established church in which creeds are repeated, sacraments administered, a liturgy performed, a clergy maintained, children catechized; everyone participates in this state of affairs and is satisfied with it. But it is dead even though the motions of life, or what seem to be such, are still to be observed.[27] It is one of the curiosities of our own day that as the secularizing process goes deeper, as the notion of a sacred order within and under which we live grows feebler, the sale of Bibles increases. One would be tempted to say something Kierkegaardian here; for example, that this represents the enjoyment of the Scriptures only at the aesthetic level, were it not for the grim fact that most of the newer versions are examples of and agents in the corruption of the language. I am reliably informed that in one of

them — in the interest of self-preservation I haven't ver-
ified this — Jesus "puts in an appearance" on the shore of
the Lake of Galilee. Such are the spurious appearances of
religious vitality.

III

We may now have reached the point where the usefulness of "form of life" begins to vanish. It was primarily a
device to show the impossibility of certain common positions in epistemology and to suggest, by offering simple
models, the role of practices in the acquiring and sustaining of a language. It is a valuable reminder of what to
look for when we try, as we may as social anthropologists,
to determine the sense of concepts employed in the
culture of relatively simple human groups. We are urged
to situate language in the manifold of culture considered
as "man's extra-somatic means of adaptation."[28] It is a
means of penetrating the "logic" of relatively isolated or
isolable practices, especially those of religious groups.
But as we pursue the criss-crossings that are required to
grasp any of the ideas and practices of the great family of
religions and quasi religions that persist in Christendom,
as we find ourselves ranging over time and space to
acquire some appreciation of the, so to speak, thickness
or density of any given idea or practice as it shows itself in
linguistic expressions or rituals, in styles of life, and in
moral and intellectual initiatives, the explanatory power
of language-game/form of life seems to vanish. It suffices
for schematized accounts or parochial instances — it is
useful in surveying the suburbs but not much use in the
great body of the city. It will still have point in the pre-
liminary analysis of some detail abstracted from the
complex mass of social phenomena. There is perhaps no
serious objection to using the expression "form of life" to
stand for religious thought and behavior in general, as
Stanley Cavell does,[29] though then it ceases to be a key to
unlock epistemological puzzles. But in so far as "form of

life" is taken as the leading clue to how we are to understand religious thought and behavior in the world religions and in civilizations, it strikes me as no more than suggestive from time to time and here and there. Further, its polemical use, against those who want to assimilate religious discourse to discourse of other kinds, tends, I believe, to obfuscation and obscurantism. I shall try to justify this presently, but before I do so, I want to say, with some fear of getting it wrong, something about Wittgenstein's aims and to suggest that Wittgensteinian fideism, even in a more defensible form than that criticized—even guyed—by Nielsen, is discordant with these aims.

The *Remarks, On Certainty*, the *Philosophical Investigations*, all seem plainly concerned with language in general, and it seems at times that while new strategies and tactics have been adopted, the basic aim of the *Tractatus*, to establish the logic of language as such, has not been abandoned. I know there are dozens of proof-texts that the devout, like their predecessors, the sectarian exegetes of Scripture, can cite that seem to make for the contrary conclusion. But the whole body of the work seems to be driving towards some kind of generality, and Wittgenstein himself seems to find his failure to achieve it a disappointment. He did not think his having produced in the *Investigations* "only an album,"[30] something necessarily connected with his method. This was "the best I could write." Fifteen years before, in November 1930, he wrote that what he was then writing was in spirit

different from the one which informs the vast stream of European and American civilization in which all of us stand. *That* spirit expresses itself in an onward movement, in building ever larger and more complicated structures; the other in striving after clarity and perspicuity in no matter what structure. The first tries to grasp the world by way of its periphery; the second at its centre—*in its essence* [my italics].[31]

This position is not without support in the *Investigations*. I find myself convinced by Mr. Hacker's argument in chapters 5 and 6 of *Insight and Illusion*.[32] The texts he adduces, and his commentary on the texts, show us that Wittgenstein's "most general and recurrent positive formulation of the task of philosophy is the claim that its purpose is to give us an *Übersicht*, a surview or synoptic view."[33] This, Hacker argues, is concealed a bit by the Anscombe translation and other English translations of the posthumous works. Of course, the tone of writing tells us that Wittgenstein saw this task as crushing and practically impossible to carry through. But to leave open the logical possibility of an *Übersicht* means that there is nothing wrong in stating the task of philosophy as that of achieving a general and comprehensive account of the language, both city and suburbs, and also new developments marked only by trenches and sewer pipes along the roads; and therefore of the world. "Grammar tells what kind of object anything is. (Theology as grammar.)"[34]

My last task is to explain why I think the use of language-game/form of life (in the discussion of religion) is sometimes something that makes for obscurantist and obfuscatory positions. In chapters 8, 9, and 10 of *Religion Without Explanation*, Phillips, with great skill and delicacy of insight, gives us some phenomenological accounts of statements about the dead and about God, as these occur within the practice, chiefly liturgical, of religious groups.[35]

He raises two important questions, one about the dead, and the other about the ascription of existence to God.

About the dead he seems to maintain the following position. To think of the dead as living, much as they are in life, but "somewhere else," is to project fantasies. This seems to be right. It seems directed against the views of spiritualists, who even tell us that Uncle Harry (or whoever) is enjoying the ectoplasmic equivalents of whiskey

and cigars, at least until he takes off for a higher plane;
and it is not what Christians seem to believe. *Expecto
resurrectionem mortuorum et vitam venturi saeculi* doesn't
seem to be about Uncle Harry agitating tambourines in
seances. But I understand him also to maintain that, for
some reason that is never made quite clear, *all* talk about
the dead, even within the religious language-game, must
not contradict the "elementary fact" that the dead truly
are dead,[36] that is, religious language of an approvable
sort expresses the significance (Phillips says "eternal
significance"—this I don't understand), for the living, of
the life that has now passed away. This seems plausible if
we consider, say, the veneration of ancestors in Con-
fucianism, but it seems odd as maintained about Christianity.

One of the best-attested facts about the history of
Christianity from about the second century onwards is
that the dead are prayed for and to; indeed, the various
forms taken by Christian eschatology from the
Apocalypse of John onwards seem to presuppose and
often to state explicitly that those who are dead pass into
another mode of existence, and that even if they rise with
Christ and in some way regain a bodily existence and with
it their identities as men, the mode of existence involved
is not that of everyday life. Why did the Protestant
Reformers put down the practice of praying for the
dead? Why did they think the practice wrong? The
answer is to be found in what they understood to be the
consequences of their doctrine of Grace, with the notions
of predestination to glory and to damnation. And they
certainly understood—how could this be denied?—
glorification and damnation as involving changes in the
mode of human existence. Belief in his foreordained
perdition drove the poet Cowper mad. If only he had
had in attendance some physician of the soul who could
have explained to him that he was making moves outside
the language-game to which these expressions belonged!

It was reserved to Dickens to find the right predicate: we are to understand propositions about God and immortality in a Pickwickian sense.

About God and his existence: much of the force of Phillips's argument comes from his taking, as central misunderstandings, the concept of God as it occurs in the works of Hume and of the Deists. (This is a natural proceeding for a British philosopher, though it may seem strange in Europe and sometimes in North America.) What is vicious here is the notion that God's existence is to be understood as the existence of an object.[37] If this were so, then the debate between the believer and the atheist would be about whether or not this object happened to exist. For an almost uncountable number of reasons this will not work out, either as theodicy or as providing a rationale of religious belief and practice. About all this one cannot quarrel with Phillips. What strikes me as odd is that he discusses the question of what it means to say that God exists as though the considerations he cites are novel, matters that had escaped attention before Hume and Kant. (He does discuss Anselm, or rather Malcolm on Anselm.) Of course, the problem of the One who is beyond all merely being thus and thus, is to be found, in an unanalyzed form, in the Old Testament, and is a standard problem in philosophical theology for the Neoplatonists and for the Scholastics. The reasons why men in the eighteenth and nineteenth centuries became insensitive to the problem, with God as a supreme regulator, a "governor" in the technical sense, or even the chairman of the board of directors, would be worth going into; I should guess that it had something to do with the state of religious life and that here at least a scrutiny of forms of life would be rewarding.

Now, Phillips's point is that it makes no sense to say that God exists because it makes no sense to say, within religious modes of discourse, that God doesn't exist; the concept of a necessary being is parasitic upon what is said in religious discourse. If one stipulates that "to exist" can refer only to objects about which it would make sense to say, even falsely, that they don't exist, then no one can have an objection, except to the usefulness of the stipulation. The stipulation strikes me as inconvenient, for since there are criss-crossings in the wide field of thought within which religious believers move, they are as likely to misunderstand "God doesn't exist" as they now, as it is believed, misunderstand "God exists" when this is said outside the religious language-game.

Two notorious features of Judaeo-Christian religious discourse seem to me to strengthen my objections to the attacks, within a philosophical context determined by the dialectic of Kant and Hume, on the notion of Divine existence. First, there is the practice of the believer in saying "Thou" to God, even if all he has to say is that truly God is a hidden God; and then there is the belief without which no one would have the courage to say "Thou," namely, that God has revealed himself. It seems to be a part of the religious language-game, as it is of most other language-games (perhaps not that of psychoanalysis), that what a man can say "Thou" to exists "over against" him, as we used to say. Consequently, Wittgensteinian fideists shouldn't be surprised if they are taken to be saying something Feuerbachian. Here is Adam Bede discoursing in that most Feuerbachian of novels:

> There's things go on in the soul, and times when feelings come into you like a rushing mighty wind, as the Scripture says, and part your life in two a'most, so as you look back on yourself as if you was somebody else. . . . I've seen pretty clear ever since I was a young un, as religion's something else besides doctrines and notions. I look at it as if the doctrines was like finding names for your feelings, so as you can talk of 'em when you've never known 'em, just as a man may talk o' tools when he knows their names, though he's never so much as seen 'em, still less handled 'em.[38]

Or here is the untheological Mr. Irwine considering the spiritual state of his flock:

> If he had been in the habit of speaking theoretically, he would perhaps have said that the only healthy form religion could take in such minds was that of certain dim but strong emotions, suffusing themselves as a hallowing influence over the family affections and neighbourly duties. He thought the custom of baptism more important than its doctrine, and that the religious benefits the peasant drew from the church where his fathers worshipped and the sacred piece of turf where they lay buried, were but slightly dependent on a clear understanding of the Liturgy or the sermon.[39]

Such are the Feuerbachian moves, to keep the scent and savor of religion, and the moral pith of it, while putting aside, perhaps sadly, "that reference to an order of goodness and power greater than any this world by itself can show which we understand as the religious spirit."[40] I don't think Wittgensteinian fideism *is* Feuerbachian, but its exponents ought, I think, to find some way of talking that makes this plainer than it is. "The abdication of belief / Makes the behavior small." So Emily Dickinson put it, happily, as so often.

NOTES

1. *Philosophical Investigations*, trans. G. E. M. Anscombe (Oxford: Basil Blackwell, 1953) I. 7, p. 5ᵉ.
2. *PI*, I. 19, p. 8ᵉ.
3. *PI*, I. 23, p. 11ᵉ.
4. *PI*, I. 25, p. 12ᵉ.
5. *An Essay Concerning Human Understanding*, III. 1.
6. *PI*, I. 111, p. 47ᵉ.
7. *PI*, I. 18, p. 8ᵉ.

8. Descartes, *Philosophical Writings*, a selection translated and edited by Elizabeth Anscombe and Peter Thomas Geach (Edinburgh: Nelson, 1954), p. 15.

9. *PI*, p. ix^e.

10. George Eliot, *Middlemarch*, Book II, ch. 20.

11. *PI*, II, xi, p. 223^e.

12. *Republic* IX, 571–72, Lindsay translation.

13. Ruth 1:15-16.

14. Ibid. 1:14.

15. Cf. D. Z. Phillips, *Religion Without Explanation* (Oxford: Basil Blackwell, 1976), p. 41 and *passim*.

16. This is also a problem for Nielsen when he tries to show that "fideism" implies "conceptual relativism" and that therefore the entire fideist enterprise self-ignites and explodes and must end in religious skepticism. He claims, for example, that the "fideist" Christian cannot find a "conflict between accepting belief system p (Christianity) as embodying the claim Christ is the truth and acknowledging that systems, q, r, t, n, m, y, s . . . are equally legitimate forms of life." (Kai Nielsen, *Contemporary Critiques of Religion* [London: Herder and Herder, 1971], p. 110.) If "Wittgensteinian fideism" implies "conceptual relativism," then the expression "equally legitimate" couldn't occur with reference to two or more language-games. I suspect that this means that Nielsen's *reductio* argument won't work just because the thesis of "cultural relativism" can't be stated coherently. It is like the argument of those who hold that logical principles are relative to particular groups of natural languages and that Chinese, for example, is non-Aristotelian. But *this* argument is stated and its conclusion is true or false. Whether or not "fideism" and "cultural relativism" can be got out of Wittgenstein's later work is another question. I am inclined to think not. Crudely, "language-game" is a heuristic device, not a constitutive principle.

17. *Kierkegaard's Attack Upon "Christendom"* (Princeton, N.J.: Princeton University Press, 1944).

18. *The Journals of Søren Kierkegaard*, selection edited and translated by Alexander Dru (London: Oxford University Press, 1938), pp. 492–93.

19. *Kierkegaard's Attack Upon "Christendom,"* p. 5.

20. Ibid., p. 6.

21. Ibid., pp. 7, 8.

22. Ibid., p. 20.

23. Ibid., p. 21.

24. *Journals*, pp. 486, 487.

25. *Either/Or*, translated by Walter Lowrie with revisions and a foreword by Howard A. Johnson (New York: Doubleday, 1959) vol. II, p. 141.

26. Walter Lowrie, *Kierkegaard* (London: Oxford University Press, 1938), p. 487.

27. I am not concerned with how far Kierkegaard was right about the Denmark of his day, but about the possibility of his having been right. That he was in fact right seems on the whole to be made plain by the present state of the Lutheran establishments in Denmark and Sweden, though not perhaps in Norway where the religious form of life is still connected with the elemental life of those who live with and from the forest and the sea.

28. L. A. White, cited in Colin Renfrew, *The Emergence of Civilization* (London: Methuen, 1972).

29. See, e.g., *Must We Mean What We Say?* (New York: Charles Scribner's Sons, 1969), p. 171.

30. *PI*, p. ix[e].

31. *Philosophical Remarks*, edited by Rush Rhees and translated by Raymond Hargreaves and Roger White (Oxford: Blackwell, 1975).

32. (London: Oxford University Press, 1972).

33. Ibid., p. 113.

34. *PI*, I. 373, p. 116[e].

35. These groups are not very well located, so that there is a difficulty about surrounding the instances of religious practice offered with other details, but they seem to be Protestant Christian groups; this is evident from the use made of 'experience', heavy with felt connections with Schleiermacher and later Protestant theologians and with, perhaps, the use of the term in William James. They would be hard to fit into Catholicism, with its *ex opere operato* view of the sacraments and its at best cautious attitude towards the affective side of mysticism. This Catholic attitude is expressed in an exaggerated way, almost as a caricature, in Pascal, both in the *il faut parier* and in what he has to say about the role of habit in sustaining and even in providing a groundwork for faith: *Pensées*, 117–29 and 474–81 (Paris: Bibliothèque de la Pléiade, 1954).

36. *Religion Without Explanation*, 136.

37. Ibid., p. 174.

38. *Adam Bede*, Book II, ch. 17.

39. Ibid., Book I, ch. 5.

40. Henry James, *Notes of a Son and Brother* in Frederick W. Dupee, ed., *Henry James: Autobiography* (London, 1966), pp. 334, 335.

Redemptive Subversions:
The Christian Discourse
of St. Bonaventure

LOUIS MACKEY

Since no one, or hardly anyone, ever fully comprehends natural forces, and since God alone knows the limits of possibility, it is frequently both dubious and presumptuous to assert that a thing is necessary. For who has ever been absolutely sure about where to draw the line between possibility and impossibility? Many ages took the following principle: "If a woman gives birth to a child, she must have had previous sexual intercourse, whether voluntary or involuntary, with someone," to be a necessary axiom. But finally, in the fulness of time, it has been shown that it is not such, by the fact that a most pure and incorrupt virgin has given birth to a child.

> John of Salisbury
> *Metalogicon*, II. 13

Love, in a world where carpenters get resurrected, anything is possible.

> James Goldman
> *The Lion in Winter*, act I, scene 4

Commenting on the first commandment, St. Bonaventure remarks: "To assert that the world is eternal is to pervert the whole of sacred Scripture and to say that the Son of God was not incarnate" (*De X Praeceptis*, II. 25). The Scriptures emplot the drama of world history from creation to apocalypse and locate its decisive *peripeteia* in the Incarnation. Aristotle's teaching, which obliterates the distinction of times in an everlasting cyclical stasis, proscribes historical development in general and thereby erases the center of history, which is marked for Christians by the cross of Christ. A *fictio mentis* of the philosophers, the doctrine of the eternity of the world is therefore one of the graven images forbidden by the decalogue.[1]

While it may be explicated in the way I have just suggested, the stark *non sequitur* of Bonaventure's predication exposes the confrontation in his writings of two descriptions of the world. The one, inscribed in the texts of Aristotle and his *epigoni*, is a self-contained and self-perpetuating system. The other, given in the text of Scripture, is dependent *ab origine* on a transcendent cause, guided from beginning to end by an external Providence, and interrupted by the intrusion of the divine into its own structures.

In his own writings Bonaventure essays to deconstruct the philosophy of Aristotle and subject it to the service of Scripture. The Christian discourse of St. Bonaventure is a signal instance of the way revelation undermines the languages by which men define themselves and of the revolutionary revision of the forms of life and language entailed by this upheaval.

I

A few paragraphs beyond the sentence I have quoted Bonaventure tells of his first encounter with Aristotle's doctrine.

> When I was a student, I heard of Aristotle that he affirmed the eternity of the world. And when I heard the reasons and arguments they were offering for this view, my heart began to pound and to think: how can this be? But nowadays these [arguments] are so evi-

dent [*tam manifesta*] that no one is able to doubt this
doctrine. (*De X Praeceptis*, II. 28)

By the second half of the thirteenth century the philosophy of Aristotle—its teachings, but even more fundamentally the logic and the vocabulary in which they are
presented—has become the normative mode of discourse at Paris, the ordinary language of the schools. St.
Bonaventure disrupts the discourse of the philosophers
by invoking the transcendent source of language: He
who speaks in revelation and is dissimulated in the
speech of philosophy.

In the *Collations on the Six Days* (XIX. 6–15) Bonaventure gives his auditors a schedule of readings and an
indication of the order in which they should be studied.
There are four kinds of books to be considered: Holy
Scripture, the writings of the Fathers, the *sententiae* of the
masters, and the books of the philosophers. Only in the
Scriptures is there salvific knowledge, for in these books
alone there is so much faith that there can be no decep-
tion.

The student of Scripture should begin by mastering
the literal sense of the text. If he provides the jar (his
capacity) and the water (his understanding of the literal
sense), God will change his water into the wine of
spiritual understanding. But a grasp of the *sensus
spirituales* is impossible without divine aid, and the student should therefore consult the Fathers, whom God
illumined so that they might open the Scriptures. And
since the Fathers themselves are difficult, the student
must have recòurse to the masters, who elucidate the
writings of the Fathers, and even to the teachings of the
philosophers, of which the masters make use. All other
writings—the Fathers, the masters, and the philosophers
—are ordered to the understanding of Scripture and
must be studied with that end in view.

But there is danger in descending to the works of the
Fathers, for they have, as Scripture does not, a beauty of

language which can deceive. There is greater danger in descending to the *sententiae* of the masters, for they contain error and misunderstanding. The descent to philosophy is the greatest danger of all. We should not "dismiss . . . the waters of Siloe, in which is supreme perfection, and go to the waters of the philosophers, in which is eternal deceit" (*In Hex.*, XIX. 12).

> There is therefore an order; man should study first Sacred Scripture, in the letter and the spirit; then the originals [the Fathers], giving Sacred Scripture priority over them. It is the same with the writings of the masters and those of the philosophers: one should study them stealthily and in passing, as if it were not good to tarry. . . . (*In Hex.*, XIX. 15)

This was Bonaventure's own curriculum, here prescribed as the proper course of study for any Christian thinker. We may interpret his admonitions with the help of a bit of speculation and some categories of criticism.

Let us suppose (though the supposition is by no means beyond question) that the primordial form of human discourse is myth. Myth—loosely speaking, stories of gods and heroes—is narrative rather than discursive. What we have come to think of as philosophy and theology originate as a dialectical critique of myth. The earliest philosophers among the Greeks either criticized myth in rational terms (Xenophanes) or attempted to replace mythic accounts of the cosmos with naturalistic explanations (the Milesian physicists). For a long while the narrative form of myth subsists alongside its dialectical/discursive counterpart. Plato's dialogues, for example, interweave myth and dialectic. In the middle ages scriptural (mythic) elements are featured and are more or less normative in philosophical and theological writing, at least until the late thirteenth century. But the tendency has been to replace myth altogether with logic and narrative with discursive writing. The history of philosophy has been the history of a massive demythologizing of the human consciousness. Contemporary philosophy is pure dialectic and its literary form discursive; at least this is the norm from which it rarely and reluctantly departs.

The philosophical critique of myth is undertaken in the interest of truth. But truth itself is defined by and in terms of this critique. In mythic narrative the question of truth does not arise because the distinction of true and false is first generated by dialectic and expressed discursively. Bards tell many a lie; truth by contrast is the discursive presentation of conceptual formulations reached through dialectical reflection. The distinction of truth and falsity is a function of the distinction between dialectic and myth, discursive and narrative forms of expression. From the beginning truth *means*, in and for philosophy, the achievement of a dialectical/discursive mode of thought and utterance. Narrative and myth are consequently relegated to literature, a realm in which (philosophers have always supposed) truth is systematically dissembled. But of course myth persists in even the most austere dialectic, as a fossil at least, and oftener than not as a structure displaced from the narrative into the discursive form and defining covertly the shape of the argument. For instance, the evolutionary philosophies of the late nineteenth century were responding to the mythic demand for origins as much as they were generalizing from the facts, replacing the creation myth of *Genesis* with a myth of science.

The history of philosophy begins with myth and moves in the direction of dialectic, from narrative through various mixed forms toward the strictly discursive essay. This is the universal analogue—the allegory—of the movement Bonaventure describes, from the Scriptures to the writings of the philosophers.[2] In terms of the fictional and thematic modes enumerated by Northrop Frye,[3] it is a movement from myth, through romance and high and low mimesis, to irony.

The Scriptures, Bonaventure says, embody supreme

perfection. They are full of faith and void of deceit. But the Scriptures are virtually mythic. Stories of God and the heroes of faith, they are as close to pure myth as anything produced by an historical (i.e., literate) people, the earlier books being in the main more perfectly mythic than the later. For Jewish and Christian thinkers they have generally functioned as the primordial origin and the ultimate point of reference, the bottom line, as it were, of theological speculation.

As mythic, the Scriptures are in narrative form. To the extent that they are mythic they have not yet conceived or effected the distinction of narrative from discursive. A mythic account is a story: a record of things said and done.[4] In myth the possibility of error has not yet been imagined, and the problem of truth has not yet arisen, because there is still no distinction between true and false. That comes with philosophical reflection. But while the truth sought by philosophers is called "correspondence" or "coherence," the passion for truth is a nostalgia for the prelapsarian unity that is presumed to antecede the division of true and false.

The patristic writings may be located in the romantic and high mimetic modes. In these texts the narrative manner, now distinguished from the discursive, still dominates. Truth, now understood as conformation to an ideal, means in this case the conformation of the patristic text to its Biblical model. The writings of the Fathers consist mostly of explication and application of Scripture. In these works there is danger of error due to their beauty. The narrative form, dominating the discursive, may violate the dialectical canon of truth in its pursuit of elegant and persuasive expression. The notion of truth as conformation to an ideal is an aesthetic definition of truth,[5] and fascination with the beauty of the conformation—Augustine is a finer stylist than Paul—can easily distract attention from the plain contours of the scriptural model.

The works of scholastic theologians are dangerous

because they contain error. The masters define truth as correspondence to fact, though in the higher realms of their theology they often revert to the aesthetic conception of truth as *convenientia*. Their writings fall in the low mimetic and high mimetic modes, dialectical concerns predominate, and the narrative is subordinated to the discursive manner. Whereas in the writings of the Fathers there was danger of error because of their beauty, in the *summae* of the masters there is actual error; both because of their remote and mediate relationship to the model and because of their reduced understanding of truth. The narrower the circumscription of truth, the more frequent the occasions of falsehood.

The works of the philosophers—of Aristotle their patron, but also the Islamic commentators and the Parisian artists—contain eternal deceit. In the ironic mode, they are at the antipodes of Biblical myth. Truth at this level means demythologizing: correspondence to fact, where fact has deteriorated from the scriptural sublime to the quotidian banal. Dialectical criticism has triumphed, and the narrative form of myth has been eliminated by a process of reductive allegorization. The supreme perfection of faith is evacuated, leaving only eternal deceit. Insofar as the philosophers take as their domain and their norm of truth the merely natural order, and insofar as they take for their method a dialectic wholly appropriated to that realm, they deceive. They deceive essentially (eternally) even when *per accidens* they tell the truth.

Intellectuals who operate in the dialectical mode, theologians are tempted to suppose that their conceptual structures are the meaning and truth of the scriptural narrative, just as philosophers have thought from the beginning that they were stating in its proper form a truth long obscured by the covering of myth.[6] That, to the mind of Bonaventure, is a condescending and calamitous error—and the rot of the "eternal deceit" of philosophy. Philosophy is in the ironic mode because the philosophers assume a position of superiority over their subject matter, which is the content of myth. Therefore, even if they tell the truth of correspondence, they deceive, for they have inverted the order of dialectical critique to mythic substance.

In terms of his own classification, Bonaventure is one of the masters. But he is also the author of the classification. (Or is he?) Bonaventure was determined to reverse, under the conditions of sophistication, the movement from myth (Scripture) to ironic rationality (philosophy): a remythologizing *reductio* to counter the demythologizing reduction of the philosophers. His constructive theology is an attempt at mythopoeia; that is, given the distinction of narrative and discursive forms, to recreate the unity of myth in the language of dialectic. The myth is scriptural, and Bonaventure's own mythopoeia is motivated and structured by Scripture. But he also takes up and tropes with the doctrines and methods of the philosophers, which in his hands become vehicles of a metaphor whose tenor is the Christian myth of redemption. By processes natural to metaphor the tenor reacts upon the vehicle, so that the language of philosophical dialectic is reappropriated to the mythic discourse of revelation. The deceptive words of men are rectified and redeemed when they are conformed to the authentic and originary Word of God.

II

The *Collations on the Six Days* opens with a commentary on the scriptural words: "In the midst of the Church he shall open his mouth . . ." (*In Hex.*, I. 1; cf. *Ecclus.* 15:15). Bonaventure identifies the *medium Ecclesiae*, the place from which a man should speak if he would speak wisely, with Christ. Christ, *medium Ecclesiae* because *mediator Dei et hominum*, holds a central position in all things (*In Hex.*, I. 1. 10):

Our intent, then, is to show that in Christ *are hidden all the treasures of wisdom and of the knowledge of God*, and that He Himself is the medium of all the sciences. He is the center in a sevenfold sense, in terms of essence, nature, distance, doctrine, moderation, justice, and concord. The first is in the metaphysical order, the second in the physical, the third in the mathematical, the fourth in the logical, the fifth in the ethical, the sixth in the political or juridical, and the seventh in the theological. The first center is first by eternal origin, the second is most strong through the diffusion of power, the third is most deep because of the centrality of position, the fourth is most clear by rational proof, the fifth is most important because of the choice of moral good, the sixth is outstanding because of the retribution of justice, the seventh is at peace through universal conciliation.

Christ was the first center in His eternal generation, the second in His incarnation, the third in His passion, the fourth in His resurrection, the fifth in His ascension, the sixth in the judgment to come, the seventh in the eternal retribution or beatification. (*In Hex.*, I. 11)

The seven moments in the history of Christ, from his generation before the creation of the world to his distribution of rewards and punishments after the end of the world, are the exemplars of theoretical and practical science. Since for Bonaventure an exemplarist explanation is an exemplary explanation, his teaching on the centrality of Christ implies a radical redefinition of the sciences.

To take but one of the seven *media*, Christ as the center in the order of doctrine: because his resurrection is the paradigm of rational proof, He is said to be the exemplar of logic. In the syllogism, declared by Aristotle to be the perfect form of argument and the normative expression of necessary truth, it is the middle term (*medium*) that does the work. By its own evidence and by its agreement with both of the extremes it compels the mind to assent to the conjunction of major and minor. Though not evident in itself, the connection of the extremes is made cogently manifest by their union in the middle (see *In Hex.*, I. 25).

Man lost beatitude because he was deceived by a diabolic paralogism. The Devil reasoned thus with Adam and Eve:

> 1. You want to be like God.
> 2. If you eat the fruit of this tree, you will be like God.

Therefore, 3. You should eat the fruit of this tree.

The major premise is true. It even has a kind of evidence, for the rational creature, which is the image of God, naturally desires to be made perfectly like Him. But the minor premise is a lie devised by Satan and backed up with the insinuation that divine jealousy inspired the prohibition of the fruit. The conclusion, eagerly embraced by Adam and Eve, follows from the premises. But one of the premises is false, the argument unsound, and the conclusion false. So perniciously false that it does not unite men to God but drives them out of Paradise into the "sufferings of nature, the needs of indigence, and the mortality of life" (*In Hex.*, I. 26).

Our protoparents were misled by a semblance of truth. The diabolic paralogism by which men are separated from God is a parody of the heavenly syllogism, which, being sound, does assimilate the rational creature to its creator. This is the reasoning of heaven:

> 1. God is eternally united with Christ.
> 2. Christ unites himself with man.

Therefore, 3. Man is united with God.

Christ is the middle term of this syllogism by which man is brought into union with God. "The major proposition existed from all eternity, the minor came about on the

cross, and the conclusion appeared in the resurrection"
(*In Hex*., I. 28). By virtue of his eternal generation the
Son is substantially identical with the Father. But He who
as God "enjoyed conformity of nature with the Father,
equality of power, and immortality of life," assumed in
his temporal incarnation the misery, need, and mortality
of fallen man and transformed them into their divine
opposites. The reality of this transformation, dissimulated in the crucifixion, was made evident in the resurrection. So God deceived the deceiver and lifted his fallen
creature to likeness with himself (see *In Hex*., I. 27–28).

The heavenly syllogism is confirmed by the postresur-
rection appearances of Christ. He enters the room
through closed doors: there is the divinity. He displays
his wounds: there is the humanity. And he elicits the
confession of Didymus: the conclusion by which man is
joined to God (*In Hex*., I. 29). And so, Bonaventure
concludes:

> This is our logic, this is our reasoning which must be
> used against the devil, who constantly argues with us.
> But in assuming the minor proposition, we must do it
> with all our strength; for we are unwilling to suffer, we
> are unwilling to be crucified. And yet all our reasoning
> is to this end, that we may be like God. (*In Hex*., I. 30)

Logic is concerned not only with truth, but also, as an
ars disserendi, with the expression and communication of
truth. Because his resurrection is the proof of Christ's
divinity and an earnest of our own, it is a conclusion
enforced by divine reasoning. In the logic of heaven it is
the necessary implication of the eternal generation, the
incarnation, and the passion of Christ. In this way Christ
by his resurrection is the center in the order of doctrine,
the middle term of all true demonstration, and the
exemplar of logic.

Bonaventure's text is obviously allegorical. But the
allegory itself is Christic. He is not explaining the resurrection in terms of the syllogism, he is expounding the

syllogism in terms of the resurrection. He is not allegorizing Christology, he is allegorizing logic. As Christ is, in the technical sense, the allegory of Holy Scripture—its central doctrine and the fundament of further spiritual meaning—and as his resurrection demonstrates this centrality, so logic, figurally and reductively, is Christology.

Bonaventure is not in the least concerned to refute the Devil by showing that his reasoning is fallacious, nor to vindicate Christianity by producing a sound argument whose conclusion is the resurrection. His diabolic argument may be unsound and his Christian syllogism valid. But that is not the point. He is using the syllogism as a terministic metaphor to figure a real union of extremes, God and man, effected by a real middle term, Christ. Syllogistic demonstration is reduced to a type of the Christian revelation, and the emergence of a conclusion from its premises is only a remote participation of Christ's emergence from the tomb.

The truth and validity of all inference is measured by its metaphoric approximation to the Christic norm. To take Aristotelian logic as the norm of argument is to commit what is for Bonaventure the original error. Aristotelian logic is a technique of sorting; the syllogism assigns particulars to classes and orders the relationships among the classes. But this presumes that the things sorted are irreducible ontic data, what Aristotle called "primary substances." Christian logic by contrast is exemplaristic. It regards things as signs in a system of signs signifying God, not things in themselves but created words in which the uncreated Word communicates itself. Things are to be read, not sorted. That Aristotle thought otherwise was a consequence of his defection from the truth of Plato. For a Christian to follow Aristotle in this matter is apostasy from revelation. Aristotelian logic can only be retained if it is taken, not as the criterion of truth and validity, but as another way of imagining the Exemplar. That is what Bonaventure attempts in his reduction of the syllogism to the truth

confirmed by the resurrection. Quite literally Christ is
the medium of all teaching, for his resurrection, as the
seal of his own legitimacy, is the paradigm of sound
demonstration.

One distinctive mark of Bonaventure's texts is their
habitual reversal of the usual senses of "literal" and
"figurative." It happens so consistently and so tacitly that
it can go unremarked by those who see something like
Aristotelian common sense everywhere. But common
sense is never more than unconscious metaphysics or
blind faith. What seems intuitively right is a view of the
world—a linguistic predisposition—devolved from assumptions made by culture and commitments so deep as
to be unfathomable. Bonaventure's subversion of Aristotelian common sense is a structural feature of his
language and therefore an index to his thought.

"Figurative" is usually opposed to "proper." Figurative
speech is improper speech, where proper speech means
the normative correlations of word, thought, and thing
warranted by Aristotelian metaphysics. Proper speech,
tied to the doctrine of primary substance, gives everything its proper name. Metaphoric naming (the principal
type of figuration) is naming by transfer, calling a thing
not by its own but by some alien appellation. The impro-
priety is justified by reference to some rule, such as
analogy, and to the purpose, usually poetic, of the discourse in which the transfer is made.[7]

All this presupposes the normativeness of Aristotle's
metaphysics and its attendant theory of language. Since
Bonaventure's exemplarism is the contrary of Aristotle's
metaphysics, Aristotle's figurative becomes Bonaventure's literal, and what is literal in Aristotle becomes
figure in Bonaventure. More accurately, there is no
"literal truth" in Bonaventure except the truth of vision,
which would be contemplative not discursive, and which
would therefore not admit the use of language at all.
Every use of language is figurative.

The only being in the full and proper sense of *esse*—a

se, *secundum se*, and *propter se* — is God. All other being stands to Him, who is imperfectly called "substance," as a relation of expression and manifestation — *a Deo*, *secundum Deum*, and *propter Deum*. Therefore the being of creatures must always be described — *properly* described — relationally, in terms of analogies, proportion, allegory, metaphor, figures of whatever sort. Every creature is literally a trope, a turning toward God.

We circumscribe God in tautologies, themselves figures of speech in this context. For what is affirmed in these tautologies is not the content intended by subject and predicate, but just the form of perfect self-identity. God is beyond representation save in that Word which is himself and in which He represents himself to himself. Only the realized contemplative, sharing in the divine life, expresses God "literally." But he does not, in this ecstasy from self, speak. This side of contemplation all we say about God and creatures alike is metaphor. For Bonaventure, therefore, Aristotle's philosophy is not the literal truth, not even about nature. Taken as such it is perniciously misleading. But the language of Aristotle can be used as a system of tropes, one among others, in which to imagine the creation.

Subverted thereby from its own point of view, the language of Aristotle is, from a Christian point of view, redeemed. The linguistic structure of common sense is deformed in order that it may be reformed in the likeness of Christ, who as Word is the Exemplar of language and as resurrected Word the *medium* of logic. Christian discourse, imitating the discourse of Scripture, should figure Christ, and "all our reasoning is to this end, that we may be like God" (*In Hex.*, I. 30).

III

I have discussed Bonaventure's attempt to re-mythologize philosophy and his reduction of Aristote-

lian syllogistic to a figure of Christian doctrine. In such
ways he hopes to deconstruct the language of philosophy
and to reconstruct it as a similitude of the Exemplar
Word. This activity of dismantling and rebuilding, which
I have illustrated from the larger members of Bonaventure's discourse, continues at the microscopic level. For
instance, the following.

   The structural unit of Aristotelian logic is the categorical proposition. And the subject-predicate form of the
categorical proposition presupposes, as a condition of
veridical representation, the ontological ultimacy and
irreducibility of primary substances: subjects that are
really subjects. Bonaventure's way of dislodging this
presupposition is to represent such substances in language that undermines their substantiality and denies
their ultimacy and irreducibility. God may be defined as
being *ex se*, *secundum se*, and *propter se*. All beings other
than God are characterized (essentially) as *ex alio*, *secundum aliud*, and *propter aliud* (*In Hex.*, I. 12). So to hang the
being of the creature on a string of prepositional dependencies, and to enfold the reality of God in a system of
reflexive relationships, is to oppose the creature as being
in alienation from itself to God as being withdrawn into
itself. And to do that is, by a twist of language, to deflect
the whole tendency of Aristotle's thought to come tò rest
in independent singulars.

   In another passage Bonaventure interprets the medieval commonplace that all beings are endowed with
mode, species, and order. Mode, he says, is that by which
a thing exists (*quo constat*), its dependence on God as
efficient cause. Species is that by which a thing is distinguished from other things (*qua discernitur*), its dependence on God as exemplar cause. And order is that by
which a thing is fitted for its end (*quo congruit*), its orienta-
tion to God as final cause. God, by contrast, is *modus sine
modo*, *numerus sine numero*, and *ordo sine ordine* (*In Hex.*, II.
23). But this demotion of things from the nominative
into oblique cases and the corresponding representation

of the Creator as a trinity of unparticipating substantives simply wipes out the doctrine of primary substance.

Bonaventure frequently asserts that creatures have three kinds of being: *esse in proprio genere*, *esse in mente*, and *esse in aeterna ratione* or *in aeterna arte* (cf., e.g., *Christus unus omnium magister*, 7; *De Scientia Christi*, 4, *corpus*; *In Hex.*, III. 8). In such contexts he normally adds that they exist most truly in the third way. A distinctive mark of the Aristotelian substance is that it does not exist *in* anything, so that to describe the being of things as Bonaventure does is by means of a particle to dethrone a first principle of Aristotle's metaphysics. And to say that things exist most truly in God is to affront Aristotle's ontology with the extremest improvement on its archenemy, Platonic exemplarism.

Minima like these, along with the cases I have developed at greater length, suggest my first and principal point: that language is both the medium and the message of Bonaventure's thought, that his subversion of philosophical language is accomplished in and by language — the language of revelation interrupting and destructuring the language of reason.

It would be possible to multiply instances indefinitely, but it is time to come to a conclusion. Let me begin to end by reemphasizing and expanding the point just mentioned, that Bonaventure's subversion of philosophy takes a linguistic form. And let me add a second and equally essential observation: that his aim is, by means of a radical decentering and relativizing of philosophical discourse, to accomplish the redemption of philosophy.

More than once Bonaventure dilates on the "errors of the philosophers." In such contexts he characteristically locates the source of these errors in the philosophers' rejection of exemplarism, beginning with Aristotle's "execration" of the Platonic Ideas (cf. *In Hex.*, VI–VII. 1–2). Recalling a common medieval notion, he describes the created world as a book, written by God and addressed to rational creatures (cf. *Brev.*, II, c. 11, n. 2).

When the rational creature fell, he lost the ability to read the language of creation and was offered a second book, the book of Scripture, written in the language of sinners. By reading the book of Scripture correctly fallen man is provided with the means of his redemption and enabled to interpret the text of creation (*In Hex.*, XIII. 12).

The principles of scriptural exegesis are also, therefore, the canons of a hermeneutic of nature (*De Red. Artium ad Theol.*, 5–7 and *passim*). The natural order is a product of the eternal art, like Scripture a book in which the divine mind expresses its exemplar Ideas. The world is *to be read*, in order that by reading it the mind of man may be conformed to the mind of God. That is what it would mean to understand the world.

By their denial of exemplar Ideas, the philosophers deny themselves the possibility of understanding the world. Their error has its root in the most catastrophic kind of misreading: the failure to read at all. Taking the world not as a text to be read, but as a collection of things to be described and sorted, they are like the man who, given a book, arranges the parts of speech in categories, classifies the letters of the alphabet by shape and size, measures the dimensions of the page, counts the occurrences of the definite article, etc. Both will amass a certain amount of knowledge—and altogether miss the meaning.

Being, at every level and in every mode, is representation. The being of God is his manifestation of himself to himself in the Holy Trinity. The being of creation is God's manifestation of himself outside himself. The reality of the world is therefore neither wholly present in the world (as Aristotle thought) nor wholly absent from it (as Aristotle thought Plato thought). The being of the world, like the meaning of any text (and being *is* meaning), is signified: everywhere always implied, never anywhere simply given. The world is a system of signs, and, like any system of signs, it both reveals and conceals the structure of signification and the transcendent *significa-*

tum. What Aristotle disdains as "poetical metaphors" (the Platonic language of participation)[8] Bonaventure magnifies as "the splendors of exemplarity" (*In Hex.*, XII. 14).

Because they misread the world fundamentally, by not reading it at all, the philosophers' discourse about reality is categorically perverse. Their language cannot tell the truth. Their principles of interpretation and their critical techniques distort the secular text and misconstrue its meaning systematically. Their own language, therefore—the discourse of *curiositas*—needs to be displaced and replaced by the discourse of exemplarism and revelation. The world *is* language, and in order to understand it one must be able to deploy a proper critical discourse: a language of interpretation that respects and reiterates the structure of the text. The subversion and reformation of philosophical language is the condition of philosophical understanding.

To the fact that the world is not substance but signification must be added the further consideration that the world is fallen. The philosophers—this is of a piece with their denial of exemplarism—take the present state of the world as its normal and continuing condition. In effect this means to take Aristotelian discourse as normative, since that discourse springs from and is designed to implement such a perception of things. But on the Christian view the world as it is is abnormal and temporary— not the world God intended, but the world man has corrupted—and the language of that world is certainly not normative. Human history, which is the history of language, obscures the divine self-manifestation. The text of creation is overwritten and effaced by the deviant and erroneous glosses of fallen humanity. Christianity will therefore insist on relativizing the Aristotelian discourse—or any mode of discourse that presupposes and institutionalizes the errors and distortions inaugurated by the fall—and rewriting the world in the language of revelation.

That was Bonaventure's program: taking the discourse of Scripture as inspired and normative, so to relativize the language of Aristotle that it may not be taken as a description of things as they are, but employed as a technique for the figural reading of the text of creation, to tear it loose from its commitment to substance and submit it to the service of signification. And on top of that, to redeem the language of unregenerate reason by transforming it into an image of the Word of revelation and restructuring it in accord with the canon of Christian doctrine. For in the redemption of the word is the redemption of the world.

In all that I have said so far I have not been concerned with the truth or the rectitude of Bonaventure's critique of Aristotle. That question could not be broached without first asking what sense may be given, in the light of Bonaventure's critique, to words like "right" and "true." It goes without saying that he would not just accept the Aristotelian definitions of these terms. It is doubtful that he would like ours much better.

I *am* concerned, however, to understand what Bonaventure is up to when he mounts his attack on the Philosopher. And to see this as itself an illustration of something more general and therefore still pertinent. Bonaventure speaks as a Christian on behalf of Christianity. As a response to revelation the Christian religion claims to derive its truth from a transcendent source. But the truth so revealed will necessarily be an interruption of human life, an intruder who, uninvited, disturbs the domestic affairs of a humanity only too eager to be at home in the —in *its*—world. The forms of life are the forms of language: the codes by which we define and constitute ourselves, which we therefore take as normative discourse representing normal existence. Christianity is a discourse of the Other that dislocates and destructures all our forms of language and their attendant forms of life. In this sense the Christian religion is not a form of life, but a deformation of language and of the life informed by that language. The reformation of life and the transformation of language projected by Christianity are available only on the other side of the collapse of all immanent norms of being and intelligibility. Christianity promises life, but the price is death. And the discourse in which the promise is made and fulfilled is intelligible only to a crucified understanding. We live by faith, which Kierkegaard describes as a certainty that embraces and sublates radical uncertainty.[9] Faith acknowledges the disjunction of God and the world and also, in response to revelation, affirms their conjunction. The sign both reveals and conceals. It implies but does not deliver its *significatum*. Faith, assenting to the signified that is always proposed but never given, is both the gap and the spark that leaps the gap. It is the *reality* of signification.

Such is the redemptive subversion intended by the Christian discourse of St. Bonaventure. Whether he is right I do not mean to decide. For my purposes in this discussion "Bonaventure" is not a proper name, but synecdoche for revealed religion. That the religion was Christian and the language it opposed Aristotelian are (perhaps) accidents of history. "Bonaventure" speaks with the voice of revelation and "Aristotle" stands (as it did in the thirteenth century) for human reason: the world as creatively spoken by the divine Logos vs. the world as comprehended in the immanent logos, the Word in which God manifests himself in us vs. the words in which we articulate our own being and project our own gods.

Revealed religion can always be explained (away) as the deviant discourse of the mentally imbalanced or the immoderate ejaculation of the too imaginative. It can even be comprehended with sympathy as the hyperbolic figuration of a truth quite respectable in itself and more or less perfectly utterable in the terms of ordinary language. But neither the writing off nor the taking in confronts the possibility of absolute alterity insinuated by revelation. Once injected into consciousness, that possibility—that an Other than ourselves, whom we could not anticipate and cannot overtake, speaks in the text of revelation—becomes a necessary structure of consciousness. Or rather, an abyss over which conscious-ness is permanently suspended and a running hiatus—a kind of perpetual stutter—of the language in which it speaks itself.

In a word: when we think of religion as a form of life, we may oversimplify. We may be led by such ways of thinking to suppose that religion is another expression of the human spirit, along with art, science, and the like. In which case we ignore the theme of every purported revelation: that true religion is not a creation of man, that the knowledge of God is given to us from a source on the other side of every immanent *Lebensform*, disturbing, reducing, and revising all such arrangements, including (perhaps especially) religious arrangements. Or, if we include the forms of revealed religion among the reli-gious forms of life, we may ignore the professed discon-tinuity of these forms with the forms in which the human composes itself, the insistent unintelligibility of revela-tion to "natural reason" and its recalcitrance to the syntax and vocabulary of ordinary language. We tend to omit the redemption altogether, or else to conceive it without the subversion that is its necessary condition.

Religion, Bonaventure reminds us, is not something with which we can ever be completely comfortable. We cannot comfortably suppose that we comprehend the content of a revelation which subverts the principles of our understanding and distorts the contours of our language. But neither may we complacently assume that we are entitled to dismiss this intruder who demands of us thoughts we cannot think and words we cannot speak. The crux of every revealed truth is the allegation that our redemption (the need for which we had not perceived apart from revelation) is effected by the actual occur-rence of that which (in human terms) is quite impossible.

That crux may be borne, but it can neither be assimilated nor deported. After all, in a world in which virgins conceive and carpenters are resurrected, it is no longer easy to know what is possible.

NOTES

1. Other Bonaventurian texts on the problem of the eternity of the world are: *Collationes de septem donis Spiritus Sancti*, VIII. 16ff.; *In Sent.*, II, d. 1, p. 1, a. 1, q. 2; *In Hex.*, IV. 13; V. 29; VI. 4; VII. 1-2; *Brev.*, II, c. 1, nos. 1-3. On the cross of Christ as the mathematical center of the world, cf. *In Hex.*, I. 21-24; also *Brev.*, Prologue, (2) and (6), 4.

2. Bonaventure's order is primarily an order of priorities and only secondarily an historical development: Aristotle obviously antedates the Fathers, the masters, and much of Scripture. But if we recall that the philosophers he talks about are in the first instance the *artistae* and their immediate sources, then the order is also historical.

3. Northrop Frye, *Anatomy of Criticism* (Princeton, N.J.: Princeton University Press, 1957), first essay.

4. In colloquial speech the request for an explanation is still often put in the form, "What's the story?"

5. In the theory of truth favored by nineteenth-century idealism, truth as conformation to the ideal of coherence becomes a purely aesthetic value — as these philosophies themselves tended toward aestheticism.

6. Cf., e.g., Aristotle, *Metaphysics*, A. 8, 1074b1-14.

7. Cf. Aristotle, *Poetics*, 21-22; *Rhetoric*, III. 2. 10-11.

8. Aristotle, *Metaphysics*, A. 9, esp. 991a21.

9. Søren Kierkegaard, *Philosophical Fragments* (Princeton, N.J.: Princeton University Press, 1962), pp. 100-103.

Belief, Change, and Forms of Life: The Confusions of Externalism and Internalism

D. Z. PHILLIPS

I. Externalism and Internalism

Wittgenstein said that "to imagine a language means to imagine a form of life" (*Investigations*, §19). Becoming acquainted with a language is not simply mastering a vocabulary and rules of grammar. It is to know how things bear on each other in the language in such a way as to make it possible to say certain things and see certain connections but not others. The same could be said for religion. It is a misunderstanding to speak of religion *as* a form of life. What can be said is that it is impossible to imagine a religion of any consequence without imagining it *in* a form of life. This insistence, under Wittgenstein's influence, in the philosophy of religion, has led to a polarizing of viewpoints in the last twenty-five years. How has this come about?

If we look back to the fifties, we find, in the literature, a certain kind of disagreement between philosophical believers and unbelievers which still persists today. The unbelievers suggested that the problematic core of religious beliefs was to be found, not in their falsity, but in their meaninglessness. The believers, on the other hand, argued that the beliefs were meaningful. By and large, however, the believers and unbelievers agreed on the criteria of meaningfulness which had to be satisfied. Under Wittgenstein's influence, some philosophers have suggested that these disputes are an irrelevance, since they never raise the question of whether the criteria of meaningfulness should be agreed on in the first place. What has happened, it is suggested, is that criteria of meaning appropriate to certain aspects of human life and activity are made synonymous with meaning as such. One obvious example in our culture has been the tendency to elevate scientific criteria and procedures in such a way. What we ought to do, by contrast, is to inquire into the meanings which religious beliefs have in the forms of life of which they are a part. Instead of constructing theories of meaning which determine what is to count as meaning, we should look at the use concepts actually have. This was the force of Wittgenstein's command, "Don't think. Look!" (*Investigations*, §66). It constitutes an attack on what I shall call *externalism*.

Following Wittgenstein's suggestions in the philosophy of religion seemed to bring problems of its own. What if we agree that various aspects of human life and activity, religion included, have distinctive meanings which must not be reduced to a spurious unity? Further, what if we also agree that philosophical confusions may be generated by the obscuring of these distinctive meanings? To some philosophers it has looked as if the inevitable consequence is that we have divided human life into strict compartments, each autonomous as far as its meaning is concerned. Religious belief, it has been said, is logically distinct from other kinds of belief. It may even be claimed that what is and what is not meaningful in this context is to be determined solely by whatever is called religious language. It may then seem that religious belief is an absolute measure brought to bear on people's lives, a measure which cannot itself be influenced, developed, changed, or threatened by events in those lives, or by social or cultural events of any kind. It would follow from such a position that religious belief would have been

made safe from all criticism and change, placed apart
from history. This being so, how could anyone be worried about its future? Future, past, or present could be no
threat to it. Faith would be independent of temporal
matters. The eternity which belonged to it would place it
above such things. So far from trying to meet the criteria
of meaning imposed on religious belief by externalism,
this reaction simply declares that all external criteria of
meaning are irrelevant to religious belief. Not unex-
pectedly, this reaction can be called *internalism*.

The price of internalism, however, is a high one. One
might well apply to internalism remarks made by F. C. S.
Schiller with respect to Kant's categorical imperative in
ethics: ". . . it could not be convicted of failure to work,
because it could never be required to work at all. Nay, it
could glory in its uselessness, and conceive it as the proof
of its immaculate purity."[1] Religious beliefs begin to look
like formal games, internally consistent, but unconnected with the day-to-day lives of men and women.

Like so many diametrically opposed theories in philosophy, internalism and externalism are thought to be the
only alternatives. In fact, each alternative feeds off the
deficiencies of the other. For example, because certain
philosophers, including myself, attacked forms of externalism in the philosophy of religion, their critics assumed
that they must hold the view I have called internalism.
Advocates of externalism, in their turn, embrace their
position because they think it necessary if the dangers of
internalism are to be avoided. I had posed the problem as
follows: "Many religious apologists feel that if religious
beliefs are not to appear as esoteric games they must be
shown to be important. . . . What remains problematic is
the way in which the apologists think the importance of
religion can be established."[2] I went on to criticize two
influential externalist attempts to achieve this. First, an
attempt to show that religious faith is more valuable than
any alternative, using 'value' as a relative term presupposing a common evaluative yardstick. Second, an at-

tempt to show that religious belief is rational, by employing a notion of rationality which transcends belief and nonbelief. I cannot repeat my criticisms of these attempts here.[3] Because I denied such external connections, critics assumed that I denied that there were connections of *any* kind between religious belief and other aspects of human life. If a man cannot support externalism, he must support internalism! Yet, textual evidence itself should have cast considerable doubt on this assumption (see Appendix).

The connections between religious beliefs and what lies around them are of mixed character. Some of the connections which are called religious may be superstitious, while others cannot be characterized in this way. This illustrates well how internalism and externalism feed off each other's deficiencies. The externalist, seeing those religious beliefs which fall under wider criteria of intelligibility and yet infringe them, wishes to stress the accountability of religion in this respect. The internalist is accused of saying that anything called religious can determine what is meaningful in this context. The internalist, on the other hand, sees the distinctive character of certain religious beliefs and does not want them to be misportrayed by the externalist's alien criteria of meaningfulness. Again, what is essential to realize is that we are not faced with a choice between these positions. In emphasizing that various aspects of human activity are autonomous as far as their criteria of meaning are concerned, it is easy, but mistaken, to deny that these various aspects are related to each other. Indeed, were it not for such relations the particular aspects could not have the distinctive meanings they do. For example, it may be confused to think that the harvest dance can be accounted for in the way one can account for the technology of the harvest. Some have thought that there was a causal connection between the dance and the harvest. In the last century writers suggested that the magical dance was a kind of primitive science. With the advent of modern technology, the day of the dance is over. The primitive assumption of a causal connection between the dance and the harvest is shown to be superstitious. We cannot argue *a priori* that this cannot be the case. Neither can we argue *a priori* that other possibilities of meaning do not present themselves. It is possible that the superstition is to be found, not in the dance, but in those who want to explain it away. The dance can be seen as a celebratory activity. Wittgenstein reminds us in his "Remarks on Frazer's *Golden Bough*" that the dance for rain occurred when rain was due.[4] There is no causal connection between the dance and the coming of the rain. If there were thought to be such a connection, would people not dance in the long months of dryness and drought? The dancers do not cause the rain to come; they greet its coming. Dancing for rain is like dancing for happiness. Thus we can mark a conceptual difference between the dance and causal technology. Having seen the difference, however, it does not follow that the dance is unrelated to its surroundings. After all, what could a harvest dance be unless there were a harvest? Rituals could not constitute the whole of human life. Therefore, if there is a relation between the harvest dance and the harvest, what happens to the harvest may affect what happens to the dance. So although no account of the dance can be given in terms of technological causality, such technology may still affect the dance. The values of technology may erode values inherent in the dance. If the values of technology become dominant and all-pervasive, the dance will come to be regarded as a waste of time.

What we have seen is that whether the meanings of religious practices are distinctive or not, one cannot ignore the relation between such practices and the human life which surrounds them. That being so, certain religiously comforting pictures have to be abandoned. It is appropriate to consider the first of these at this stage in the paper. I shall consider the others later. One might call the first comforting picture that of *religious individualism*. It appears to be something like this:

Christianity does not belong to the world of time. It is part of the eternal. The eternal cannot be dependent on the temporal. Therefore, whatever happens in the secular culture which surrounds us, Christianity is eternally safe. There is a direct relationship between the believer and his personal Savior. The believer who is saved has certainty in his heart. Whatever happens about him, the heart, the secret place, is safe from such influences. He does not have to worry about what happens to personal relationships, the family, the society, or the culture, since the communion between the heart and the Savior is direct, beyond the influence of personal, family, social, or cultural events. Is not Heaven beyond the earth, and does not God in His Heaven see to it that the faith of the faithful is not frustrated? Therefore the nature of faith is beyond historical or cultural influences, since that faith is made secure by a transcendent cause, by no less than divine causality itself.

That is the comforting picture of religious individualism. But, as I have said, it is a picture which must be put aside. There is no necessity about the continued existence of Christianity. There is nothing in the nature of the universe, as it were, which guarantees this. There was a time before the existence of anything called a Christian culture, and there could be a time when it has disappeared from the face of the earth. It is this possibility that the comforting picture of religious individualism will not allow. According to the comforting picture, Christianity is safe in the believer's heart. The meaning is internal, beyond the reach of social or cultural influences. But does this make sense? What if someone suggested that Sarah, Abraham's wife, longed for the liberation of women in the sense in which this is widely sought in America today? The answer, of course, is that it is mean-

ingless to attribute such longing to Sarah. It is meaningless because such ideas were not part of her world. But
what if someone wanted to argue that the longing was
independent of all this, something internal in Sarah's
heart? Would not the answer be that the possibility of a
secret thought, even in the depths of the heart, depends
on the limits of intelligibility within the culture? The
limits of intelligibility determine possibilities of speech
and thought. This is as true of secret thoughts as of
public utterances. So you could not have a longing to be
king in a culture where the notion of kingship has no
meaning. In the same way, Sarah cannot long for that
which has no meaning for Sarah. This is not to argue
against new developments or radical changes. Such developments and changes cannot be understood *in vacuo*,
but must be seen against the background or in the
context of the events in relation to which they occur. For
these reasons, we cannot argue that Christianity has a
hiding place in man's heart, since if the culture declines,
there will also be a decline in the thoughts of men's
hearts.

But what of God's activity? Is not such activity beyond
all cultural boundaries? If the assumption is that God is
some kind of object beyond the world who operates
causally, according to His will, on the world, the assumption is again a confused one. God's reality and His
divinity are synonymous. God is divinely real; He is not
real in any other sense. The nearest thing to God or grace
in the secular world is luck or fate.

II. Religious Belief and Cultural Change

For all these reasons, the comforting picture of religious individualism has little substance. The Word cannot dwell among men no matter what the state of the
culture in which they live. Awareness of this fact has led
many to ask today, "What are we to do about the future of

religion?" meaning, it seems, "How can we make sure that religion has a future?" It seems to many philosophers that these questions can only be answered if one can show that religious belief is more worthwhile or more rational than any alternative in terms of some common measure of worthwhileness or rationality. In the absence of a common measure, how can there be *alternatives* to religious belief? How can belief be threatened, lost, or replaced, if one denies the availability of such a measure? There is no simple answer to this question, but a number of possibilities which may arise serve to clarify the issue.

As we have seen, I have already denied that a firm religious belief means a belief firmly grounded according to the common measures mentioned. Because of such a denial, J. R. Jones asked me the following question: ". . . when belief is . . . undermined, or weakened, it then looks as though the picture itself begins to lose its hold on the life of the believer. And I wonder what this really signifies?"[5] The answers I gave to this question are, I believe, important in the context of our present problem. They can be divided into four kinds of response: First, I drew attention to the ways in which rival secular pictures constitute threatening alternatives to religious faith. Second, I indicated some of the ways religious faith may be mischaracterized in face of such threats. Third, I spoke of cultural changes which may erode religious belief. Fourth, I asked what could be said if these changes were so pervasive as to destroy religious belief. It would be useful to elaborate on these four responses in order to appreciate the different contexts in which questions about the future of religion may arise.

First, then, I spoke of rival secular alternatives to religious faith. I had in mind here, principally, what religious believers would call temptations. These are present in any age insofar as most religions have called men away from certain activities and attitudes which are called sinful, unholy, or unclean.[6] The philosophical

difficulty for some philosophers has been to see how
these can be assessed by a common measure. And, yet,
should there be any difficulty? Consider the following
example. There is a gentleman who appears advertising
cigars on television. No sooner does this immaculate man
light up his cigars than women come from all quarters to
gather round him. We can imagine people reacting in
certain moods by saying, "What a man!" Here, 'man' is
clearly not a purely descriptive term. They are extolling,
praising, wondering. A cluster of images influences their
attitude: success, flair, charm, panache, the great
seducer, etc. At the heart of Christianity is a very different event. It is that of a torn body on a cross. Here, too, it
was said, "Behold, the man!" Do we need anything other
than these two images to explain why they should be at
war in the human soul? Once we elaborate their content
we see how they cannot coexist in peace within the same
person. We do not need anything apart from these two
visions, one of self-aggrandizement and the other of
self-abnegation, to see why they generate conflict. The
Christian will speak of the temptations of the flesh, while
the pagan may complain of "priests in black gowns
walking their rounds and binding with briars" his "joys
and desires." But from whichever direction the threat is
thought to come, that one threatens the other cannot be
denied. It seems as if we only have to expound the cases
for the conflict to become obvious.

Yet, should we say that the conflict is obvious? There is
no harm in this as long as one remembers that there are
certain conditions within which it appears obvious. In
other words, that the conflict appears obvious at a certain
time, does not mean that this reaction cannot be changed
or eroded. I said that as soon as we expound the rival
conceptions the tension between them becomes apparent, but it must not be forgotten that in expounding them
thus two conditions are implied: (a) that the state of
society or culture is such as to enable such an exposition
to be made; (b) that the exposition does not fall on

completely barren ground. The exposition, even if not
heeded, is at least recognized. Given these conditions, it is
fairly easy to see how a religion may speak to the culture
which surrounds it. The prophets of the Old Testament
provide abundant examples of what I have in mind.
They say, "Thus saith the Lord . . ." and then proceed to
rebuke people or nations for their evil ways. They call the
wanderer back to a straight and narrow path. What is
said from a religious point of view here at least has the
possibility of being heard. It points out that covenants are
being broken or disregarded, the tradition misrepre-
sented, or it points to possibilities of creative extensions
of the tradition to meet new situations.

Second, in face of threatening secular alternatives,
religious beliefs may change their character. From the
beginning Christianity develops an *apologia* to meet the
challenges which come from varieties of unbelief. A
certain aspect of a culture, for example its science, may
enjoy such prestige that the religious apologist may feel
that he ought to be able to give an account of religion in
the same terms. Matters become complicated when a
particular *apologia* becomes a substantive part of faith for
the believers. If such an *apologia* is not necessary to the
faith, the faith becomes a mixture of the meaningful and
the meaningless. The spiritual may become superstitious. For example, if what is important is conceived in
terms of the ability to control, it may be difficult to think
of other conceptions of importance. Religious belief may
be advocated in the same terms. Religion, it is said, will
give one the most extensive control of all over one's life.
Indeed, it gives one control over what happens to one
after death. It provides eternal security as distinct from
temporal security.

Dominant conceptions of control may make it difficult, if not impossible, to see religious reactions for
what they are. We have already seen the way in which
some writers thought that the harvest dance was causally
related to the harvest. They were blind to the celebratory

character of the dance. Ironically, if the confused account enjoys sufficient prestige, the adherents of the
dance may also come to think that unless the dance is
causally efficacious it has no point. Confused reactions by
believers to external threats may, in this way, distort and
even erode the character of religious belief.

At this point we need to consider the third context in
which cultural changes may affect the character of religious responses to human life. I have in mind changes
which cannot be said to be the fault of any single individual. Let us consider some examples. First, consider the
effect of the development of birth control on the notion
of life as a gift from God. How is it possible for believers
to regard the birth of a child as a gift from God, while at
the same time they urge their children to take advantage
of contraception? How is it possible for believers to thank
God for the birth of their child if they have been trying to
plan it to the day, if possible, to take advantage of tax
benefits? Perhaps it *is* possible, but at least there is a
tension, a question to be resolved, since the notion of
planning and that of a gift seem to be in conflict here.
There is a danger of the religious words, even if they are
used, seeming empty in the mouths of the believers.
Again, religious responses may be eroded in seemingly
more innocuous ways than this. It might be thought that
traffic congestion has little to do with conceptions of
death, apart from death on the road. Yet, this is not so.
Think of the ways in which the dead were accompanied
to their graves. People walked with them to the end.
They shared a last journey with them. Despite carriages,
no one except the infirm thought of doing anything but
walking. Then came the car. At first all seemed well. Even
if people no longer walked, it was a solemn procession,
one which pursued its way slowly and which no other
traffic would cut across. As the car became economically
within the reach of more people, wider roads were
needed. Traffic congestion and the laws it generated
became a problem for the solemn procession of the dead.

The procession went faster, and the increased speed eroded the solemnity. Car drivers no longer thought it necessary not to break the funereal procession. Slowly, but surely, factors which at first seemed to have little to do with religion eroded a religious response. With the coming of cremation, the mourners knew that they were not really there at the end anyway. Whereas earth is thrown on the coffin in their presence at a burial, everyone knows that the bodies are not cremated during the cremation service. How soon before it will be asked why, since we are not there at the end, we take the body anywhere? Why not have it collected and taken to a central store from which it could be dispatched economically and hygienically?

Consider a final example in this context. Could hills declare the glory of God once gold has been discovered in them? Well, they might. The gold may be regarded as untouchable no matter how great the needs of the people. But if the hills are mined, could the hills declare the glory of God? Again, they might. If the hills are only mined in face of real need, the hills might come to be regarded as the Great Providers. But what if the hills are mined because of the greed for gold? It is hard in these circumstances to see how the very same hills could declare the glory of God, since the act of exploitation, the utilitarian attitude to the hills, would jar with regarding the hills as belonging to God.

These examples may bring us to see why a second religiously comforting picture has to be put aside. The picture I have in mind may be called that of *religious rationalism*. It appears to be something like this:

No matter what cultural changes may take place, the validity of religious belief is secured by formal arguments which transcend the relativity of cultural contexts; arguments such as the ontological argument, the cosmological argument, and the argument from design, all of which prove the existence of God. Reason is one, and transcends the kinds of considerations appealed to in this essay. Such considerations cannot affect the truths of reason where the existence of God is concerned.

As a matter of fact, I believe the exact opposite of this conclusion to be the case. So far from it being the formal proofs which gave a rational foundation to the beliefs of the faithful, it was the lives of the faithful which breathed into the formal proofs whatever life they had. At a time when nature could be looked at as God's creation, when the heavens declared His glory, it is not hard to see how the intellectual expression of this religious response could take the form of an argument from design. The argument will not do. It is a poor shadow of what it is trying to express, but that it is trying to express it is the sole justification for its existence. Norman Kemp Smith suggests that this is why Hume and Kant, despite having exposed the formal inadequacies of the argument, kept thinking it worthy of the greatest respect when they turned to look at nature itself.[7] Similarly, at a time when the whole world could be seen as God's creation, it is not surprising that the attempt to express this intellectually could take the form of the cosmological argument. Faced with the formal inadequacies of the proof, some Neo-Thomists suggested that one could only understand the inference from world to God if one stood within, or took for granted, the cosmological relation.[8] Understood formally, this introduced a vicious circularity into the argument, since the cosmological relation is one of the things the argument is meant to establish. Nevertheless, the insight contained in the Neo-Thomistic suggestion lies in the appreciation of the religious response as logically prior to the attempt at intellectual elucidation. In his discussion of the ontological argument, Norman Malcolm has suggested that philosophers have thought the expression "necessary existence" meaningless because they have ignored the human phenomena which give rise to the expression.[9] O. K. Bouwsma finds the argument to be "the language of praise cooled down for purposes of proof" and finds the home of the derived expression "that than which none greater can be conceived" in the language of praise in the Psalms and elsewhere.[10]

From these considerations, one can see how the comforting picture of religious rationalism must be put aside. If the argument from design, the cosmological argument, and the ontological argument are attempts to give intellectual expression to the way nature may tell of God, the way the world can be seen as God's creation, the way God can be thought of as eternal, respectively, the arguments could not survive the demise of these religious reactions. Without the religious responses, the intellectual arguments would be no more than empty shells.

With the decline of these religious responses, we face a situation rather different from the first context in which we discussed mere deviations from the responses. There, as we saw, it made sense for the prophet's word to be a word of rebuke, a word of warning. In the present examples, we are discussing a context in which such rebukes would not mean anything. If a word of rebuke or warning is heard here, it is not a reminder of what they know already, but a new word for their critical time.

The fourth context concerning religion and culture is one in which not even a prophet or a lonely visionary could be found. There would be no believers at such a time. Compare the absence of love in Aldous Huxley's *Brave New World*. Human relationships are spoken of in terms of sensation and transient need, much as if wine were being discussed. One might say to someone about to taste a second glass of wine, "I wouldn't drink that if you've had some of that other kind. You need something different in between." In Huxley's world one would say, "If you've just had sexual relations with him or her, I wouldn't advise that one next, you need something different in between." Of such a time one could say with J. L. Stocks that "the convenience of a utensil would be the highest form of praise."[11] Here, in terms of the language available, the possibility of love is ruled out. What could a word in the service of religion mean here? Clearly, there could not be a word *in* time in such a context. But might there be a word out of time, the beginning of a new possibility? This is a question to which I shall return later.

III. Religious Belief and the Future

The examples I have considered, needless to say, are not meant to be any kind of historical or social survey, but are simply illustrations of the various relations between religious belief and conceptual change.[12] If we remember what we have said about the necessity for a connection between the Word of faith and various features of human life, and about the ways in which faith may be eroded, we can see that we are at the same time discussing religion's application to reality. Asking whether religion has any application to reality in the future, is asking whether religion can speak to the future, whether it has anything to say. If religion has nothing to say, it has no future. True, its nominal existence may outlast its actual or authentic existence, but when that happens, religion is an edifice which, though standing, stands condemned. Many religious apologists are reluctant to countenance these possibilities. They take refuge in a third religious comforting picture, one I shall call, *religious accommodation*. It appears to be something like this:

So far we have seen that there is a close connection between religion and culture. Without such a connection, religious beliefs would be formal practices of little significance. So there is no such thing as bare Christianity. From the beginning, Christianity responds to the culture surrounding it. Therefore, whatever the changes in our culture, however dark it becomes for certain religious traditions, Christianity can always accommodate the situation by taking on new cultural forms. If there is no such thing as bare, cultureless Christianity,

Christianity can wear a new culture as it disposes of the previous one like an old garment. The question for Christianity in our day, therefore, is of how to come to a new cultural form which would contain an acceptable *apologia* to meet our contemporary crises.

What of this argument? It is a tempting thesis, but one which, I believe, like the two comforting religious pictures we have already considered, must be put aside if confusion is to be avoided. First, the relation between Christianity and culture is unlike the relation between a body and clothes. Although clothes may be changed, the identity of the body remains the same. But Christianity does not wear culture like a garment. Christianity is part of the culture; sometimes the most important part. Further, if we want to speak of a Christian tradition, there cannot be a complete break between the different periods in the history of the Faith. If we raise the question of God's identity, this has nothing to do with referring to an object. We did not learn the word 'God' in that way. We would determine whether two people are worshiping the same God by looking at the ideas which enter into their worship. So if we want to say that we worship the God of Abraham, Isaac, and Jacob, there must be enough to link us with the past to enable us to claim that we are worshiping the same God. Yet, although this conceptual continuity is important, we cannot assume that this continuity can be guaranteed in any situation. This brings us back to the question of whether such continuity can be safeguarded in our day.

When believers see religious belief declining it is natural that they should long for some kind of reawakening. There is nothing misplaced in such a desire. What is misplaced is the thought that such an awakening could be made a matter of policy by the Church. If such a policy were possible, no doubt there could be discussions within the Church about the cultural forms which ought to be adopted in face of contemporary crises. But such discussions would harbor deep confusions.

What is the source of the confusion? Does it not consist
partly in this: If there is a relation between religion and
culture, and if the religious element expresses what is
spiritual, it is important to realize that the religious
element is a *contribution* to the culture and not simply a
reflection of it. For example, Michelangelo's work does
not reflect or illustrate religious ideas, but contributes
towards such ideas. Similarly, Beethoven could not have
given us the last movement of the Ninth Symphony
unless there were conceptions of joy in human life. But
Beethoven does not reflect those ideas; he contributes to
them by extending them. To see how he does this we
would have to speak about the last movement of the
Ninth. What is deep in a culture did not come about as a
matter of policy. Shakespeare, Beethoven, and Tolstoy
did not give us their work *in order* that we might have
something excellent in the culture. No, they gave us what
they had to give and we found it was excellent. Perhaps
the point can be clarified as follows: Some time ago
British universities were asked whether they wanted to
be centers of excellence, as if that question made sense. A
university does not become a center of excellence by
trying to be one. On the contrary, we are fortunate if
scholars give themselves to their subjects as best they can.
The results may or may not be excellent.

Religious apologists have much to learn from these
conceptual truths. The Church cannot speak to the culture in which it is placed by making this a matter of policy.
No, it speaks and perhaps the consequences will be good.
The Church cannot *decide* to speak with authority
in the culture. It speaks and perhaps its voice will be
authoritative. Jesus spoke as one having authority, not as
one who decided to speak with authority. This is simply
one instance of a wider truth. A movement, and a religious movement is no exception, flourishes when people
are engaged in its particular concerns, not when they are
preoccupied with its maintenance. One is characteristically concerned about maintenance, how to keep going,

for example, in a marriage, when there is a threat of things falling apart. But, it may be said, things are falling apart, so why should not the Church be concerned with maintaining the faith? This form of words, in certain circumstances, may be unobjectionable. Even if they are not sufficient conditions for religious renewal, there are many social, political, and cultural developments which the Church may recognize, with good reason, either to be or not to be in its interest. Yet, the matter must be stated carefully. There is nothing in religion akin to carrying on for the sake of the children in a marriage. What one must notice is that in the marriage example one settles for second best, but in the case of religion there is no second best once the spirit of faith has departed. One can have integrity in a marriage when love has died, but there is no such thing as integrity in religion when faith has gone.

The misconception comes from the way in which the religious apologist thinks a word in time may be found as a matter of policy in the time of crisis or in order to avert a crisis. Consider a parallel example.[13] After the horrors which the Jews suffered at the hands of the Nazis, many Jews have vowed that such a thing shall never happen again. Such a reaction is understandable. Money was given to a university to conduct research into the reasons why the Nazis did what they did, and into the conditions for the rise of Nazism. The hope is clear. They thought that if such reasons and conditions could be determined, men could see to it that such atrocities did not occur again. There is confusion in this natural hope. What is needed in order to withstand such a possibility is a moral reaction and probably force of arms in the end. The moral reaction cannot be secured by a quasi-scientific enquiry. Similarly, if one were looking for the authoritative voice of the Church in our day, it would have to take a spiritual form; that is, and this is a matter of logic not of apologetics, the mode of the message must be as spiritual as its content. If an authoritative voice is heard it will be the voice of a new prophet, or perhaps something will be

shown authoritatively through some events which may
befall the culture. The confusion is in the religiously
comforting picture which suggests that any cultural shift
can be accommodated by religious apologetics as a matter of policy.

We have considered the relation between religion and
culture in various contexts. A word may speak within a
tradition, checking, warning, or rebuking. Religious
apologetics may distort religious belief in its attempt to
meet threatening rival alternatives to religious belief.
These alternatives may erode religious belief. At times, a
tradition may be extended creatively to meet a crisis.
Think of the way in which a word in time was needed
during the Babylonian Exile. The people asked how they
could sing the Lord's song in a strange land, and there had
to be an extension in the notion of the divine before the
question could be answered. Yet, here, the language of
faith, creatively extended, can still speak to the people.
Finally, we considered a situation such as that depicted in
Huxley's *Brave New World*, and raised the question of how
faith could speak in it. Clearly, from what we have seen,
philosophy cannot argue for an *a priori* religious optimism
or an *a priori* religious pessimism in face of these facts.
Nevertheless, some philosophical insights can be gained in
seeing why this is so.

One of the most difficult problems to which religion
has to speak is that of the problem of evil. Apologetics
often takes the form of tired theodicies which try to
justify evil in terms of some greater good.[14] It is essential
to recognize the pointlessness of many forms of evil, to
realize that there is no reality, no scheme of things, which
owes us one kind of treatment rather than another. This
acceptance of the pointless in the work of Sîmone Weil
leads to a certain conception of grace. She talks of a
recognition that nothing is ours by right; that all things
are a gift from God. In others, recognition of the
pointlessness of suffering has led to protest, rebellion, or
a conception of the absurd. I cannot elaborate these

views here. I call attention to Simone Weil's views simply in order to make a difficulty clear. If we allow her view, which for many, I know, would be to allow too much, God being with the believer is intimately connected with the realization of grace in face of the pointlessness of evil. It is connected in her work too with what she calls love of the beauty of the world and the necessity of fighting against those relations and conditions which she believes militate against this beauty being revealed. It is in contexts such as these that she speaks of Christianity offering a use for suffering but no remedy for it. Although Jesus calls out on the cross, "My God, my God, why hast thou forsaken me?" experiencing the void, the pointlessness, he was able to commit himself into his Father's hands. Yet, does evil always allow room for this reaction? Simone Weil acknowledges that there can be affliction of such extremity that even the possibility of a cry is ruled out. The human becomes a vegetable. How does the death of Jesus speak in this case, since, as I have said, Jesus was not deprived of the ability to cry out? Consider examples from the two extremes of the human spectrum. What of the baby thrown up and caught on the bayonet? What of the incomprehension of the senile? In the one case, conditions do not exist in which what Simone Weil would call 'being with God' can be realized. In the other case, these conditions have deteriorated beyond recall.

I am not saying that the words "Yea though I walk through the valley of the shadow of death I will fear no evil for thou art with me" *could not* mean anything in these circumstances, but it is difficult to see what they *do* mean. It is one thing to see one's own sufferings in relation to God's will and quite another to see other people's sufferings in that way. Clearly, if we are to say that God is in the sufferings of others, especially in the extreme cases I have indicated, this cannot mean that the sufferer is aware of God's presence. Here, it seems to me, there is an important distinction between what can be *said* in suffering and what can be *shown*. This is not an easy distinction to uphold in all circumstances, since often what suffering shows is the destruction of what is fine and the creation of meanness and pettiness. Yet, this is an area in which dogmatism is singularly out of place. All I can do is to offer an example. In one of his early works, *Night*, Elie Wiesel tells of the deportation of Elisha and his young family from their village in Eastern Europe to Auschwitz and Buchenwald. In these horrific circumstances Jews had to face a crisis of faith. What could it mean now to speak of themselves as God's chosen people? Wiesel writes of three hangings at Auschwitz, one of them involving a child. His reaction is impressively ambiguous:

> The SS seemed more preoccupied, more disturbed than usual. To hang a young boy in front of thousands of spectators was no light matter. The head of the camp read the verdict. All eyes were on the child. He was lividly pale, almost calm, biting his lips. The gallows threw its shadow over him.
>
> This time the Lagerkàpo refused to act as executioner. Three SS replaced him.
>
> The three victims mounted onto the chairs.
>
> The three necks were placed at the same moment within the nooses.
>
> "Long live liberty!" cried the two adults.
>
> But the child was silent.
>
> "Where is God? Where is He?" someone behind me asked.
>
> At a sign from the head of the camp, the three chairs tipped over.
>
> Total silence throughout the camp. On the horizon, the sun was setting.
>
> "Bare your heads!" yelled the head of the camp. His voice was raucous. We were weeping.
>
> "Cover your heads!"
>
> Then the march past began. The two adults were no longer alive. Their tongues being swollen, blue-tinged.

But the third rope was still moving; being so light, the child was still alive . . .

For more than half an hour he stayed there, struggling between life and death, dying in slow agony under our eyes. And we had to look him full in the face. He was still alive when I passed in front of him. His tongue was still red, his eyes were not yet glazed.

Behind me, I heard the same man asking:

"Where is God now?"

And I heard a voice within me answer him:

"Where is He? Here He is — He is hanging here on this gallows . . ."

That night the soup tasted of corpses.[15]

If words or events can speak of God even in the face of the sufferings of others, those words or events will have the authority which comes of spirituality. To think that philosophical analysis as such could be the source of such authority would be to misconstrue the whole of this paper. If a philosopher thought otherwise it would be a comic presumptuousness on his part. Yet, it must be said that this presumptousness can often be found in the realm of religious apologetics. The construction of tired theodicies is a case in point. Many would say that the language of faith shows this tiredness more generally in our culture. No statement on a large scale seems possible. The search for a religious syntax in the New English Bible has led to a loss of authority in the language.[16] There can be no *a priori* optimism about our ability to restore this deficiency. This is what Beckett shows us in *Krapp's Last Tape*. Beckett's character tries to make a new tape:

Now the day is over,
Night is drawing nigh-igh,
Shadows—(coughing, then almost inaudible) of the
    evening
Steal across the sky

He fails. He throws the new tape away and puts an old tape on once more to capture a moment of passion long ago. But there is no comfort to be found there either:

> Here I end this reel. Box—(pause)—three, spool—(pause)—five. (Pause). Perhaps my best years are gone. When there was a chance of happiness. But I wouldn't want them back. Not with the fire in me now. No, I wouldn't want them back.

Beckett's character is "motionless staring before him. The tape runs on in silence."

There is nothing new to say. It's too late to bring the past back. That is one lesson, at least, that Beckett's character has learned—"But I wouldn't want them back. . . . No, I wouldn't want them back." The present a failure, and the past gone—"The tape runs on in silence." This is a difficult lesson for religious apologists to accept. Yet, it would be difficult to deny that religion faces dark times, at least in the English-speaking world. The language offered is tired and inadequate. Efforts on a wider scale fail.

In such a context it is essential to put aside the three religiously comforting pictures we have considered: religious individualism, religious rationalism, and religious accommodation. This does not mean that the Church has no important task in such dark times. On the contrary, it has the task of being a *via negativa*: the task of exposing pseudoprofoundity and of attacking empty attempts to fill the void created by the loss of religious authority. In all conscience, there are plenty of such efforts to exercise the Church's vigilance. Unfortunately, many of them come from the Church itself. It seems as though anything is allowed on the tape as long as it is recorded in the name of Christianity. If such things are accepted, if this is what is to be on the tape, it will be the only language available to us. If this is to be the limit of our language, this will be the limit of our world too.

Yet, it must be remembered that if *a priori* optimism

cannot be justified, neither can *a priori* pessimism. It is tempting to conclude that if such a time as Huxley's *Brave New World* came about, religious faith would be impossible, since the conditions from which it could sustain itself are lacking. This reaction is mistaken. For any religious reaction we may care to think of, we can imagine cultural changes which would deprive it of the surroundings in which it flourishes. Yet, the philosopher has no right to infer from this that religious responses will not take new forms. Philosophers may say that in such-and-such a cultural context a particular religious belief could have no sense, but they cannot say that no kind of religious belief would be possible. Such *a priori* pessimism is unfounded. New forms of religious belief may arise. What we have seen is that these cannot be made a matter of policy. When Beethoven's music arrived it was possible to see connections between it and the tradition he inherited. Yet his coming could not have been predicted on the basis of such a tradition. Similarly, if a new prophet were to come, we would see a host of connections between his words and the state of our society and culture. But, again, this does not mean that we can foresee his coming on the basis of our present situation.

On the other hand, there can be no necessity about such an awakening. Perhaps in the future the tape is to run on without any mention of Christianity. If this came to pass, the situation would be at a further extreme from that depicted by Beckett, since no one would know that there had been anything religious on the tape in the first place.

Finally, we must ask why so many apologists find such conclusions disturbing. They feel that there is some kind of contradiction involved in saying that the eternal truths of religion may pass away from the face of the earth. For obvious reasons, such a prospect is a terrible one for believers, but is it one that contradicts their faith? Some would think so. Has not the eternal become dependent on the temporal? Sociologists would have us believe that "sociology uncovers the infinite precariousness of all socially assigned realities,"[17] and that that revelation casts doubt on the absolute status of any values. Can one still speak of religious truths as eternal in face of these considerations?

The answer is that we can, because the considerations harbor confusions. If what is required in order to make religious truths eternal, in the sense of nonprecarious, is to make their continued existence in a culture secure, immune from all contingencies, I hope I have said enough to show why such a requirement cannot be granted. In this context, religious truths are as precarious as anything else. This does not mean that the beliefs are any less absolute or eternal in the sense this has in religion. It is possible, given the grammar of such beliefs, to say something now about a time when no one believed in God. The believer can say that such a world has turned its back on God, or that God has judged such a world by ceasing to reveal himself in it. The absolute demands which belief makes on believers, the way the character of the beliefs as eternal truths expresses the turning away from worldliness to spirituality, none of this would be less true for a believer because the majority, or even all mankind, ceased to believe in such things. After all, that is not why the believers put their trust in these truths in the first place.

In the Fifth Book of *The Prelude* Wordsworth discusses his fear that the whole world of learning might be destroyed. Even if this were to happen, he believes new awakenings of creativity would occur. What is of interest, however, is the effect on the status of the works even if they are destroyed. He longs for the existence of these works among men to be made permanent and wonders

> . . . why hath not the Mind
> Some element to stamp her image on
> In nature somewhat nearer to her own?
> Why, gifted with such powers to send abroad
> Her spirit, must it lodge in shrines so frail?

Similarly, believers may wonder why the truths of their faith are in earthen vessels. Yet, Wordsworth does not confuse the question of the extent of human allegiance with the character of the learning he extols. When he thinks of poetry and geometry this is how he speaks of them:

> On poetry and geometric truth,
> And their high privilege of lasting life,
> From all internal injury exempt
> I mused.[18]

The lasting life which is exempt from all internal injury has clearly nothing to do with continued duration. It has to do with what geometry and poetry are capable of expressing. The "eternity" found in these contexts is not the same as that which religions talk of. Nevertheless, in religion too it is important not to confuse "lasting life," in the sense of surviving contingencies, with what is expressed by religious truths. It is in this latter context, if at all, that sense can be made of an eternity "from all internal injury, exempt." To seek exemption from external injury, too, is to seek, in the interests of a confused conception of eternity, what cannot be obtained.

APPENDIX: SOME TEXTUAL REFUTATIONS

It has been said by many who have criticized Wittgenstein's influence on the philosophy of religion that this has led to a rigid compartmentalizing of different aspects of human life. As a result, religion has been cut off from all other aspects of human life. The present paper shows that this is not so. It has been said, however, that the views I express *now* are simply a consequence of realizing the inadequacies of my earlier views. Since this is said again and again in print and in discussion it may be useful (but it may be optimistic to think so) to present some textual evidence to the contrary.

In recent literature we can find at least five theses which have been attributed to me from time to time:

1. Religious beliefs are logically cut off from all other aspects of human life.

2. Whatever is called religious belief determines what is and what is not meaningful in religion.

3. Religious beliefs cannot be criticized.

4. Religious beliefs cannot be affected by personal, social, or cultural events.

5. Religious belief can only be understood by religious believers.

None of these theses are mine. Let us look at some textual evidence.

It is true that in "Religious Beliefs and Language-Games" in 1970 I said,

> I write this chapter as one who has talked of religious beliefs as distinctive language-games, but also as one who has come to feel misgivings in some respects about doing so.[19]

But this confession was premature. Recently, I said of it:

> In face of familiar objections to philosophers of religion influenced by Wittgenstein I recently underwent the self-inflicted penance of re-reading what I had said on these topics. I found no evidence of my having said that faith could not be challenged or overthrown by non-religious factors. On the contrary, the account I gave of prayers, for example, would make no sense without connections with features of human life intelligible independently of religion. . . . I suspect that we have heard so-called fideistic (a term which, unfortunately, has come to stay) views attributed to us so often that we have almost come to believe in their accuracy ourselves without checking it.[20]

But the criticisms are not accurate. Consider the following:

1965: Religious concepts, however, are not technical concepts; they are not cut off from the common experiences of human life: joy and sorrow, hope and despair. Because this is so, an attempt can be made to clarify their meaning. The idea of prayer as talking to God presents us with this task. (*The Concept of Prayer*, p. 40)

1967: I am anxious to show that religion is not some kind of technical discourse or esoteric pursuit cut off from the ordinary problems and perplexities, hopes and joys, which most of us experience at some time or other. If it were, it would not have the importance it does have for so many people. By considering one example in detail—namely, eternal love or the love of God—I shall try to show what significance it has in human experience, the kind of circumstances which occasion it, and the kind of human predicament it answers. ("Faith, Scepticism and Religious Understanding," in *Faith and Philosophical Enquiry*, p. 21)

1966: It seems to me that the religious concepts discussed by Professors Hick, Hepburn and Ramsey have been abstracted from the human phenomena that lie behind them, and so have lost or changed their meaning. ("Religion and Epistemology: Some Contemporary Confusions," in *Faith and Philosophical Enquiry*, p. 143)

1966: I am not arguing for a sharp separation between religious discourse and moral discourse. I cannot accept the account offered by some theologians which makes religion appear to be a technical language, cut off, alien and foreign to the language spoken by everyone else in the community. This picture is false and misleading. It cannot account even for religious phenomena, such as the traffic between unbelief and belief. . . . Religious doctrines, worship, ritual, etc., would not have the importance they do were they not connected with practices other than those which are specifically religious. When a man prays to God for forgiveness, for example, his prayer would be worthless did it not arise from problems in his relationship with other people. These problems can be appreciated by the religious and the non-religious alike. Because of such connections between religious and non-religious activity, it is possible to convey the meaning of religious language to someone unfamiliar with it, even if all one achieves is to stop him from talking nonsense. ("God and Ought," in *Faith and Philosophical Enquiry*, p. 230)

1968: Religious believers make mistakes like anyone else. What they say, *if* it comes under the appropriate criteria of meaningfulness, must answer to these criteria. Hick is right too in saying that certain conceptions of God are confused, e.g. "Yuri Gagarin's concept of God as an object that he would have observed, had it existed, during his first space flight." It can be shown to be confused in two ways: first, by reference to what one can reasonably expect to observe in space, and secondly, by reference to what is meant by the reality of God. ("Religious Belief and Philosophical Enquiry," in *Faith and Philosophical Enquiry*, p. 72)

. . . consider whether religious language-games could be the *only* language-games played. Could they constitute the whole of a language? If not, why not? This raises interesting and important questions about the relation of religious language-games to *other* language-games. (Ibid., p. 75)

1970: It is important, however, not to confuse the view I have argued for with another which has superficial resemblances to it. The view I have in mind was one put forward by T. H. McPherson: "Religion belongs to the sphere of the unsayable, so it is not to be wondered at that in theology there is much nonsense (i.e., many absurdities); this is the natural result of trying to put into words — and to discuss — various kinds of inexpressible 'experiences,' and of trying to say things about God."[21] J. A. Passmore comments on this observation: "One difficulty with this line of reasoning, considered as a defence of religion, is that it 'saves' religion only at the cost of leaving the door open to any sort of transcendental metaphysics — and indeed to superstition and nonsense of the most arrant sort."[22] . . . Religion must take the world seriously. I have argued that religious reactions to various situations cannot be assessed according to some external criteria of adequacy. On the other hand, the connections between religious beliefs and such situations must not be fantastic. . . . whether the connections are fantastic is decided by criteria which are not in dispute. For example, some religious believers may try to explain away the reality of suffering, or try to say that all suffering has some purpose. When they speak like this, one may accuse them of not taking suffering seriously. Or if religious believers talk of death as if it were a sleep of long duration, one may accuse them of not taking death seriously. . . . The religious responses are fantastic because they ignore or distort what we already know. . . . When what is said by religious believers does isolate the facts or distort our apprehension of situations, no appeal to the fact that what is said is said in the name of religion can justify or excuse the violation or distortion. ("Religious Beliefs and Language-Games," in *Faith and Philosophical Enquiry*, pp. 93–99)

This is just a small sample of the textual counterevidence I could produce in face of the five theses in the philosophy of religion which have been attributed to myself and others. Why, despite such evidence, do these theses persist? Why is it probable that they will continue to persist? Part of the answer, I believe, is as follows:

Many philosophers of religion influenced by Wittgenstein have spent much of their time denying that connections of a *certain kind* hold between religious beliefs and other aspects of human life. Similarly, they have denied the appropriateness of *certain kinds* of criticisms of religion. Those who have been criticized often react as follows: "This is what I mean by the connection between religion and other aspects of human life and this is what I mean by criticism of religion. Here is Phillips and others like him denying the intelligibility of such connections and criticism. Therefore Phillips and others like him hold that there is *no* connection between religion and other aspects of human life and that religion cannot be criticized." Of course, all that I and others have denied is *their* conception of the relation between religion and other aspects of human life and *their* conception of criticism of religion. Sometimes, the explanation of the persistence of the critical theses concerning Wittgenstein's influence in the philosophy of religion I have outlined is as simple as that.

NOTES AND REFERENCES

1. F. C. S. Schiller, *Problems of Belief* (London: Hodder and Stoughton, 1924), pp. 138–39.
2. "Religious Belief and Language-Games," in *Faith and Philosophical Enquiry* (London: Routledge and Kegan Paul, 1970), p. 80.
3. Ibid., pp. 79–92.
4. Ludwig Wittgenstein, "Remarks on Frazer's *Golden Bough*," trans. A. C. Miles and Rush Rhees, in *The Human World*, no. 3, May 1971.
5. J. R. Jones and D. Z. Phillips, "Belief and Loss of Belief," in *Faith and Philosophical Enquiry*, p. 115.
6. Ibid., p. 116. I say most religions because, as Simone Weil points out, there are religions which deify what is dear to many men, namely power and control. These religions she calls anthropomorphic and naturalistic. See my book *The Concept of Prayer* (London: Routledge and Kegan Paul, 1965), p. 101 f.

and p. 158. Also see "On the Christian Concept of Love," in *Faith and Philosophical Enquiry*, pp. 247–48.

7. Norman Kemp Smith, "Is Divine Existence Credible?" in *Religion and Understanding*, ed. D. Z. Phillips (Oxford: Basil Blackwell, 1967), p. 107 f.

8. E. L. Mascall praises A. M. Farner's remarks in *Finite and Infinite* where he says "There is no question of demonstrating God from the creatures by a pure inference. God, being a unique existent, must be apprehended if he is to be known at all. But . . . he must be apprehended in the cosmological relation" (quoted in *Existence and Analogy* [London: Longmans, 1949], p. 69).

9. Norman Malcolm, "Anselm's Ontological Argument," in *Religion and Understanding*, p. 61.

10. O. K. Bouwsma, "Anselm's Argument," in J. Bobik, ed., *The Nature of Philosophical Inquiry* (Notre Dame, Ind.: University of Notre Dame Press, 1970).

11. J. L. Stocks, "Desire and Affection," in *Morality and Purpose*, ed. with an Introduction by D. Z. Phillips (London: Routledge and Kegan Paul, 1969), p. 40.

12. I have explored some of the relations between philosophical analysis and conceptual change in "Philosophers, Religion and Conceptual Change," in J. King-Farlow, ed., *The Challenge of Religion Today* (New York: Canadian Contemporary Philosophy Series, Science History Publications, 1976), pp. 190–200.

13. I owe this example to Frank Cioffi.

14. For an extended account of these objections see *The Concept of Prayer*, chapter five and my paper, "The Problem of Evil" and "Postscript" in S. Brown, ed., *Reason and Religion* (Ithaca, N.Y.: Cornell University Press, 1978).

15. Elie Wiesel, *Night*, trans. from the French by Stella Rodway in *Night, Dawn, The Accident* (London: Robson Books, 1978), pp. 71–72.

16. See Ian Robinson, "Religious English," in *The Survival of English* (Cambridge: Cambridge University Press, 1973).

17. Peter Berger, *Invitation to Sociology* (London: Penguin Books, 1975), p. 178. The alleged implications of this remark are discussed in my paper, "Alienation and the Sociologising of Meaning," *The Aristotelian Society*, supp. vol. LIII, 1979.

18. I am grateful to my colleague, Mr. D. L. Sims, for suggesting in discussion the parallels in the work of Wordsworth and Beckett.

19. *Faith and Philosophical Enquiry*, p. 78.

20. "Postscript," in *Reason and Religion*, pp. 138–39.

21. T. H. McPherson, "Religion as the Inexpressible," in A. Flew and A. MacIntyre, eds., *New Essays in Philosophical Theology* (London: S.C.M. Press, 1955), p. 142.

22. J. A. Passmore, "Christianity and Positivism," *Australasian Journal of Philosophy*, 1957, p. 128.

Religion and Groundless Believing

KAI NIELSEN

I

It is a fundamental religious belief of Jews and Christians that a human being's chief end is to glorify God and to enjoy Him forever. Human beings are not simply creatures who will rot and die, but they will survive the death of their present bodies. They will, after the Last Judgment, if they are saved, come into a blissful union with God, free finally of all sin, and they will be united in Heaven in human brotherhood and love. But for now, that is, in our "earthly" condition of life, we stand in division both inwardly as self-divided creatures and against each other as well; a kingdom of heaven on earth is far from being realized. We humans—or so Jews and Christians believe— are sinful creatures standing before the God of mercy and of love whose forgiveness we need and to whom everything is owed.

The thing to see here is that being a Jew or a Christian is not just the having of one framework-belief, namely a belief that there is a God. And it is not just, as some philosophers seem to assume, the having of that belief and the having of another, namely that we will survive the death of our bodies. Rather, as Wittgenstein and Malcolm stress, what we have with a religion is a system, or as I would prefer to call it, a cluster of interlocking beliefs, qualifying and giving each other sense and mutual support.[1] We have here a world-picture which

93

not only tells us, or purports to tell us, what is the case but
orients and guides our lives and can touch profoundly —
if we can accept such a world-picture — our hopes and
expectations as well. To be a Jew or a Christian is to be a
person whose sense of self and sense of the meaningfulness of life is tied up with that world-picture.

It has seemed to many philosophers, believers and
nonbelievers alike, that key concepts in this world-
picture — God, heaven, hell, sin, the Last Judgment, a
human being's chief end, being resurrected and coming
to be a new man with a new body — are all in one degree
or another problematic concepts whose very intelligibility or rational acceptability are not beyond reasonable doubt. Yet it is just this skeptical thrust — or so at
least it would appear — that Wittgenstein and certain
Wittgensteinians oppose as itself a product of *philosophical* confusion.[2] In the systemic home of various ongoing
and deeply entrenched language-games, these concepts
have a place, and in that context they are, and must be,
perfectly in order as they are. Within those language-
games no genuine questions of their intelligibility or
rational acceptability can arise and criticisms from the
outside — from the vantage point of some other language-game — are always irrelevant, for the criteria of
intelligibility or rational acceptability are always in part
dependent on a particular language-game.[3] It might be
thought that the phrase "genuine question" in the above
is a tip-off marking what in effect is a *persuasive* definition
and showing, as clearly as can be, that such questions can
and do arise over such general criteria within the parameters of such language-games. But the response would be
that no one who commanded a clear view of what she or
he was saying and doing would try to make such a
challenge or search for such general criteria of intelligibility or rationality, for she would be perfectly aware that
she had no place to stand in trying to gain such a critical
vantage point. There just are no criteria of intelligibility
or rationality *Überhaupt*.[4] Such a person has and can have

no Archimedian point in accordance with which she could carry out such a critique.

Genuine criticism, such Wittgensteinians argue, will have to proceed piecemeal and within the parameters of these different but often interlocking language-games. Critique, if it is to cut deep and be to the point, must be concrete (specific) and involve an extended examination of the forms of life from *within*. For such a criticism to be a genuine possibility the critics must have a sensitive participant's or participant-like understanding of these forms of life as they are exhibited in the language-games with which they are matched. (Perhaps it is more adequate to say the language-games are embedded in forms of life!)

In such a context criticism is in order and is an indispensable tool in the *development* of a tradition, but there is — so the claim goes — no genuinely relevant criticism possible of language-games as a whole or of forms of life. There is no coherent sense, such Wittgensteinians argue, in which we can speak of a confused language-game or an irrational form of life or of a full-fledged, conceptually distinct practice which is irrational or incoherent.[5] Our language-games are rooted in these practices and are not in need of justification or of a foundation. In fact the whole idea of foundations or grounds or justification here is without sense. Foundationalism is a philosophical mythology. There is no logic which can give us the *a priori* order of the world. Rather our logical distinctions are found in or become a codification of distinctions found in our various language-games. But the sense — the intelligibility — of our language-games cannot be coherently questioned. There is, they claim, no coherent sense to the phrase "a confused language-game" or "a confused but conceptually distinct practice" or "an irrational form of life." We indeed have a deep philosophical penchant to go on to question, to ask for foundations for, to try to justify such practices, language-games, or forms of life. But it is just here that we fall into transcendental

illusion. We do not recognize the import of Wittgenstein's full stop and we dream of justification where none
exists or even could exist.

Both understanding and genuine criticism must, initially at least, proceed by seeing how the various concepts
interlock and how in the form of a whole system—a
cluster of concepts—they make sense. There is no understanding them in isolation. We come to understand their
use by coming to see their place—their various roles—in
the system. There is no understanding "the chief end of
man" outside of something like a religious context and
there is no understanding the distinctive end of man
envisioned by Christianity without understanding its
concept of God. And there is no, so the claim goes, even
tolerable understanding of Christianity's concept of God
without understanding the Christian concept of the end
of man and man's highest good. And in turn to understand that, it is necessary to make sense of a man's
surviving the death of his present body and coming to
have a resurrection body in a resurrection world. There
is no more breaking away the Christian conception of the
end of man or man's highest good from such cosmological conceptions than there is a way of breaking away the
conception of the Last Judgment from them. And in turn
the concepts of heaven, blissful union with God, human
brotherhood, love, and sin do not stand on their own feet
but gain their distinctively Christian sense from their
interlocking with these other concepts of Christian life.
These concepts and many others like them cluster together, and we cannot understand them in isolation.
Moreover, they stand and fall together.

II

Yet, these crucial Wittgensteinian points notwithstand-
ing, there is a certain probing of those concepts which
is quite natural and which can—or so it at least ap-

pears—be carried out in relative isolation from the examination of the other concepts of the cluster, provided we have something like a participant's grasp of the whole cluster. We, in wondering about the resurrection body in the resurrection world, naturally wonder how identity is preserved in the switch or in the resurrection or reconstitution of the body. Who is it that is me in the interim between the decay of the "old body" and the emergence of the "new" one, and in what space and in what world in relation to our present familiar world of everyday life and physics is this resurrection world? Is it even logically or conceptually possible for a rocket to be shot up to it? Somehow this all seems fatuous—a plain getting of it wrong—but what then is a getting of it right, what is it that we are talking about, and does it make sense? Does it help our understanding at all to say that we must just understand it in its own terms? Does it help particularly the perplexities we feel at this juncture to relate such conceptions to the other conceptions in our religious language-game? It is not at all clear to me that, about these particular worries, it does help much, if at all, to relate these philosophically perplexing conceptions to other religious conceptions.

Even more important is the role of the concept of God here. While gaining its meaning in a certain determinate context in a cluster of concepts, the concept of God can still have, in relative isolation, certain questions addressed to it. We glorify God and find our chief joy in Him, but *who* or *what* is this God we enjoy and how appropriate is the use of personal pronouns in such talk? We have the word 'God' but is it a proper name, an abbreviated definite description, a special kind of descriptive predicable or what? It surely appears to be some kind of referring expression, but what does it refer to? How could we be acquainted with, or could we be acquainted with or otherwise come to know, what it stands for or characterizes? How do we—or do we—identify God, how do we individuate God, what are we talking

about when we talk of God, do we succeed in making any
successful reference when we speak of God? What or
who is this God we pray to, love, find our security in,
make sense of our lives in terms of, and the like? Our
cluster of religious concepts will help us somewhat here.
We know He is the God of love who transcends in His
might and mystery our paltry understanding. *Some* Jews
and Christians believe He is that being whom we will
somehow meet face to face when we are resurrected and
our sins are washed away, and we know that He is a being
of infinite mercy and love with whom we may somehow,
someday, be in blissful union in a world without division,
strife, or alienation, where love and brotherhood (sister-
hood) prevail. This helps to some extent to locate God in
conceptual space but only to some extent, for still the
nagging question persists: *what* is it or *who* is it that is this
being of infinite love, mercy, power, and understanding
of whom we stand in need? What literally are we talking
about when we speak of this being or what kind of reality
or putative reality do we speak of when we speak of or
even talk to God? (If we have no conception of what it is
to speak literally here, then we can have no understanding of the possibility of speaking metaphorically or
analogically either, for the possibility of the latter is
parasitic on the possibility of the former.) Suppose
someone says there is no reality here and 'God' answers
to nothing at all—stands for, makes reference to, nothing
at all. How are we to answer him and show he is mistaken? And how are we to answer the other chap who
looks on the scene and says he does not know how to
decide such an issue? He does not understand what it
would be like to succeed in making reference with 'God',
but not knowing that, he also does not know—indeed
cannot know—that 'God' does *not* stand for anything
either. If we don't understand what could count as
success, how could we understand what could count as
failure? All these people can play Jewish or Christian
language-games with such a cluster of concepts, but they

remain thoroughly perplexed about what, if anything, they are talking about in speaking of God. If that is so, how can we possibly be justified in saying that the concepts in question are unproblematic and are in order as they are? We know what it is religious people do with such words; we can do similar things with words as well, and we understand full well the uses of language involved. We could do it all quite competently in a play if necessary. But though we can speak and act and at least seem to share a common understanding, we cannot decide whether 'God' does, or even could (given its meaning), secure reference—stand for something, refer to something actually real, and we do not agree about or understand how to go about settling or resolving or even dissolving that issue. But how then can these key concepts or conceptions be unproblematic?

III

Some, whom I have called—perhaps tendentiously—Wittgensteinian Fideists, would respond that the core mistake in what I have been arguing is that I continue to construe God as an object or a thing or entity of some sort. That this is a governing assumption for me, as it is for Flew as well, is revealed in my and his repeated request for a specification of the referent (denotation) of 'God', in our asking repeatedly *who* or *what* is God.[6] We both are, it could be argued, looking for the substance answering to the substantive and sometimes at least that is a mistake of such an order as to show a fundamental confusion about the logic of God. It confuses the surface grammar of the concept with its depth grammar.

There is no more question, they claim, of finding out whether God exists than there is of finding out whether physical objects exist. The putative question "Is God real?" makes no more sense than does the question-form "Do material objects exist?" It is true that a man who rejects religious belief and does not believe in God is not cut off from reason—is not thereby shown to be irrational—as is the man who does not believe there are any physical objects. Indeed we would not know what to make of a child's doubting the reality of physical objects, but we would understand very well a child's not believing in God or an adult's coming not to believe in God. The kind of unquestionable propositions that Moore and Wittgenstein take to be bedrock unquestionable propositions may, in their normal employments in normal contexts, very well be propositions it really makes no sense to question. They are framework beliefs. Whatever other differences they may exhibit, they are propositions which are not, or at least so these Wittgensteinians claim, *testable empirically* and thus are, in that way, not grounded in experience.[7] There is no finding out whether they are true or false. The fact that the basic teachings of religion cannot properly be called knowledge should cease to be paradoxical, shocking, or perplexing when we reflect on this and on the fact that these various framework beliefs—certain of them as we are—are still not bits of knowledge. Moreover, that is not distinctive of religion and ideology but is a feature, as Wittgenstein shows, of many quite unproblematic domains as well.[8] All language-games have their framework propositions and, as they are something we cannot be mistaken about or in any way test or establish, they are not bits of knowledge. Doubting, establishing, believing, finding out, and knowing are activities which only make sense within the confines of language-games, and they require each other for any such single activity to be possible. But such contrastive conceptions cannot be applied to the framework propositions themselves. And while it is perfectly true that cultural changes can and do bring about changes in what we do and do not regard as reasonable, what realism requires, Wittgenstein argues, is a recognition that we do not have and cannot come to have a historical vantage point which will tell us what, such historical contexts apart, is "really reasonable."[9] (Indeed such talk may very well have no coherent sense.) What we have in various areas are different and often incommensurable beliefs which are, for many at least, unshakable beliefs which regulate their lives. But there is no finding out which, if any of them, are really true. There is, such Wittgensteinians argue, no establishing "philosophical foundations" which show that some or all of them have a rational underpinning. Such rationalist hopes are utterly misguided.[10]

To understand what we mean by 'God', to grasp its role in the stream of life, is to come to understand its role in such religious activities as worship, prayer, and the praise of God. That is where we come to understand what it is that we believe in when we believe in God. That is where the experience of God will have some reality, and it is in those surroundings that "Thou art God" has a clear sense. There God becomes a reality in our lives, and it is there where it becomes clear to us that the existence of God is neither a theoretical nor a quasi-theoretical nor even a metaphysical question. We respond, if we are religious, to religious talk, and on certain appropriate occasions some of us even sing out "God is our God above all other Gods." Some Wittgensteinians have even claimed that "God exists" in its actual logical form (its depth grammar) is not something which actually is, as it appears to be, in the indicative mood. Most definitely, such Wittgensteinians claim, it is not a statement of fact or even a putative statement of fact. 'God', they also claim, is not a term concerning which it makes any sense at all to look for its referent. In Christian and Jewish language-games "God is real" is a grammatical truth.

IV

These claims deserve a critical reception. "God is unreal. God is but a figment of our imaginations borne of our deepest needs" are not deviant English sentences. There are a number of language-games in which such talk is quite at home. But as believers don't speak that way, it will be claimed that the above skeptical utterances are not at home in religious language-games. (But again, believers could act in a play and speak that way or write novels, as Dostoevsky did, in which characters say such things.) At least some believers understand such talk and there are many ex-believers and doubting Thomases and people struggling in various ways with religious belief. In their struggles and in their expectable and understandable wrestlings with faith, such talk has a home. Questions about whether God is really a figment of our imagination quite naturally arise. Moreover, their typical contexts are not the bizarre and metaphysical contexts in which we can ask whether physical objects are real or whether memory beliefs are even reliable. In our lives, that is, they are, for believer and nonbeliever alike, not idling questions like "Is time real?"

It might be responded that it is necessary to recognize that for a medieval man asking "Is God real?" would be such an idling metaphysical question. Perhaps that is so—though that would have to be shown; after all, Machiavelli was a late medieval man—but, whatever we should say for the medievals, what is true in cultures such as ours is that such questions repeatedly arise in non-philosophical contexts where the engine is not idling. Why are they not in order in those contexts? What grounds have we for saying they are not real doubts or that they would never be asked by anyone who understood what he was asking? That some people—even that many people—do not question these propositions does not show they are "unquestionable propositions." That they are plainly not *just* theoretical questions does not show that they are not theoretical at all. Perhaps changes over time and, in our culture, about what is taken to be reasonable and what is not, have changed our responses to these questions and our attitudes toward worship, praise, and prayer? But then we need to recognize just that and consider what that involves and what philosophical significance it has.

It is indeed true that we need an understanding of God-talk to understand the sense of sentences such as "I take my illness as a punishment," "Your sins are forgiven," "God is merciful to sinners," and "He has experienced God's mercy," but we also need, to understand them properly, to see how they fit into a system. (We can speak of a "system of salvation" and we need not think of it as a theoretical system.) But none of this precludes or makes unnecessary asking about the referent (alleged referent) of 'God'. Granted 'God' does not stand for an object among objects, but still what does 'God' stand for? None of the above has shown that to be a pseudo-question.

V

Wittgensteinians—as is most evident in the work of Winch, Dilman, and Phillips—try very hard to avoid facing that issue. Indeed they struggle to show that in reality there is no such issue at all.[11] I have tried to expose the nerve of some of the issues here and to maintain against them that there appears at least to be a real issue here.

Wittgensteinians will contend that language-games and forms of life are neither well-founded nor ill-founded. They are just there like our lives. Our understanding of them and assurance concerning them is shown by the way we go on—by how we employ them—whether we claim, in our philosophical moments, to understand them or not. There is no showing that the evaluative conceptions and norms, including the norms of reasonability embedded in them, require a justification, a foundation, or even an explanation. Indeed, if they are right, the first two are impossible and even the third (i.e., that they require explanation) may be impossible as well, but, impossible or not, such things are unnecessary. The urge to attempt such justifications and explanations is very deep—as deep as the very subject that has traditionally been called "philosophy." But Wittgenstein schools us to resist this urge. If he is near to the mark, reason—the use by human beings of the various canons of rationality—requires that we resist it. Such general inquiries about religion and reality are senseless. There neither is nor can be a *philosophical* underpinning of religion or anything else. But such philosophical foundationalism is not needed. It is not something the loss of which undermines our capacity to make sense of our lives. Bad philosophy gives us the illusion that religion requires such a foundation and sometimes succeeds in so infiltrating religious conceptions that they do come to have incoherent elements which should not be accepted. Good philosophy will help us spot and excise those nonsensical, metaphysical elements. But when purified of such extraneous metaphysical elements, religious belief is both foundationless and not in the slightest need of foundations or of some philosophical justification.

I do not intend here to rise to the fundamental metaphilosophical issues raised by this Wittgensteinian rejection of the search for "philosophical foundations." Such a way of viewing things is plainly less popular now than when Wittgenstein and some of his followers first pressed it home. Yet it seems to me that philosophers have not so much answered it, or shown it to be a pointless lament, as simply to have ignored it. I think that this is a mistake and that a philosophical practice that survives taking this challenge seriously will look very different indeed from the practices that went before it.

However, I don't want to speak of that grand issue here but only to face some of its implications for religion, if one takes to heart Wittgenstein's critique of the pretensions of philosophy. I agree, of course, that religion can have no such philosophical or metaphysical foundations.

I do not even have a tolerably clear sense of what it means to say that there is some *distinctive philosophical* knowledge that would give us "the true grounds" of religious belief. I am no more concerned than are the Wittgensteinians to defend such a metaphysical religiosity and I am not concerned to replace it with some distinctive atheological "*philosophical* knowledge."

However, our perplexities and difficulties about God and religion are not just in a second-order context where the engine is idling. Most of them are not like perplexities about how we can know whether there is an external world or whether induction is justified or whether our memory beliefs are ever reliable. It is not just the talk about God-talk that perplexes us but certain central bits of the first-order talk itself. People with a common culture and a common set of language-games are very much at odds over whether we can know or justifiably believe that there is a God and this can be, and often is, linked for some with an intense desire to believe in God or, for that matter (though much less frequently), not to believe in God. It is common ground between myself and Wittgensteinian Fideists that we do not think that there is any metaphysical Santa Claus that is going to provide us with answers here, to wit with some distinctively "metaphysical knowledge" which will assure us that there is or is not, must or cannot be, that putative reality for which 'God' is the English term.

Using their own procedures, procedures I take within a certain scope to be perfectly proper, I started by looking at religious language-games we all can play and concerning which we at least have a knowledge by *wont*. When we look at certain religious language-games and — indeed from inside them — put questions which are perfectly natural, questions that plain people ask, and ask without suffering from metaphysical hunger, we will see that perplexities *arise* about to whom or to what we could be praying, supplicating, or even denying when we talk in this manner. Where 'God' is construed nonanthropomorphically, as we must construe 'God' if our conception is not to betray our belief as a superstition, it appears at least to be the case that we do not understand who or what it is we believe in when we speak of believing in God. It is not just that we do not understand these matters very well—that is certainly to be expected and is quite tolerable—but that we are utterly at sea here.

Such considerations make skepticism about the reality of such a conception very real indeed. And that very skepticism—as Dostoevsky teaches us—can even come from someone who has a genuine need or at least a desire to believe. That skepticism is common enough and, if I am near to my mark, could be well-founded, even in complete innocence of or in utter irony about philosophical foundations for or against religious belief.

NOTES

1. Ludwig Wittgenstein, *On Certainty*, trans. Denis Paul and G. E. M. Anscombe (Oxford: Basil Blackwell, 1969) and Norman Malcolm, "The Groundlessness of Belief," in Stuart C. Brown, ed., *Reason and Religion* (Ithaca, N.Y.: Cornell University Press, 1977), pp. 143–57.

2. Wittgenstein in *On Certainty* and again in a somewhat different way in his *Philosophical Investigations*. See Rush Rhees, *Without Answers* (London: Routledge and Kegan Paul, 1969); the article cited in the previous note from Malcolm; D. Z. Phillips, *The Concept of Prayer* (London: Routledge and Kegan Paul, 1965), *Death and Immortality* (New York: St. Martin's Press, 1970), *Faith and Philosophical Enquiry* (London: Routledge and Kegan Paul, 1970) and *Religion Without Explanation* (Oxford: Basil Blackwell, 1976); Ilham Dilman, "Wisdom's Philosophy of Religion," *Canadian Journal of Philosophy*, vol. V, no. 4 (December, 1975) and "Wittgenstein on the Soul," in G. Vesey, ed., *Understanding Wittgenstein* (London: Macmillan, 1974).

3. In addition to the above references, note as well Peter

Winch, "Understanding a Primitive Society," in Bryan R. Wilson, ed., *Rationality* (Oxford: Basil Blackwell, 1970) and "Meaning and Religious Language," in Stuart Brown, ed., *Reason and Religion*.

4. See the above references to Phillips and Winch and, most centrally, Wittgenstein, *On Certainty*. I discuss further facets of this in my "Reasonable Belief Without Justification," in *Body, Mind and Method: Essays in Honor of Virgil C. Aldrich*, Donald Gustafson and Bangs L. Tapscott, eds. (Dordrecht, Holland: D. Reidel, 1979).

5. Most of the above references are pertinent here but note, as well, D. Z. Phillips, "Philosophers, Religion and Conceptual Change," in John King-Farlow, ed., *The Challenge of Religion Today* (New York: Neale Watson Academic Publications, 1976), pp. 190–200.

6. See my *Contemporary Critiques of Religion* (New York: Herder and Herder, 1971) and my *Scepticism* (New York: St. Martin's, 1973), and see A. G. N. Flew's *God and Philosophy* (London: Hutchinson, 1966) and A. G. N. Flew's *The Presumption of Atheism* (New York: Barnes and Noble, 1976).

7. Norman Malcolm, "The Groundlessness of Belief."

8. Ludwig Wittgenstein, *On Certainty* and G. H. von Wright, "Wittgenstein On Certainty," in G. H. von Wright, ed., *Problems in the Theory of Knowledge* (The Hague: Martinus Nijhoff, 1972), pp. 47–60.

9. Wittgenstein, *On Certainty*, pp. 43 and 80.

10. Again, *On Certainty* seems to me a crucial reference here. See also Stanley Cavell, *Must We Mean What We Say?* (New York: Charles Scribner's Sons, 1969).

11. Such accounts have been powerfully criticized by Robert C. Coburn, "Animadversions on a Wittgensteinian Apologetic," *Perkins Journal*, Spring 1971, pp. 25–36, and by Michael Durrant, "Is the Justification of Religious Belief a Possible Enterprise?" *Religious Studies*, vol. 9 (1971), pp. 440–54 and in his "Some Comments on 'Meaning and Religious Language,'" in Stuart Brown, ed., *Reason and Religion*, pp. 222–32.

A Perceptual Model of Belief in God

KENNETH SAYRE

According to his biographers, Wittgenstein was listed as Roman Catholic on his military records, later spent time as a gardener in a monastery, vigorously defended religion against positivistic disparagement, and at the end of his life received a Catholic burial. Yet those who knew him did not consider him a believer, and apparently he did not so consider himself. Referring once to a pair of students who had become Roman Catholics, he said he could not possibly believe all the things they believe. And in his lectures on religious belief, he professed himself unable to understand what it is to believe in a Final Judgment.

But perhaps he merely disagreed with his students' brand of Catholicism, found the imagery of the Final Judgment hard to interpret, and made a practice of keeping his religious beliefs to himself—yet devoutly believed in God from beginning to end. Biographical matters aside, the story could be rounded out in many different ways, some making him a believer and others not.

Nonetheless, we might find it natural to insist, either he did or did not believe in God. That is, if we set about patiently to find the fact of the matter, then the fact is there for us to discover. To sympathize with this view, we have only to assume that 'God' refers to a certain unique entity, that 'believing in' designates a mental attitude one holds toward such entities, and hence that 'believing in

God' picks out a state of affairs that either does or does not obtain for a given person. In effect, according to this view, mankind divides into believers and nonbelievers, much as it divides into male and female. The only interesting question about whether so-and-so is a believer is the question about which subgroup so-and-so belongs to.

Now it seems to me that this view is wrong in almost every respect. To explain why is the burden of the first part of this paper.

I

To begin, let me suggest another way of drawing the story together, which initially seems more faithful to the historical Wittgenstein. Although he frequently spoke of God in conversation and writing, and possessed the awe and wonder of many religious believers, he never was certain what the term 'God' designates, or whether it designates anything at all. In the *Tractatus*, moreover, belief is a relationship between matters of fact from which God, being transcendental, would be excluded. Although Wittgenstein in later years relinquished this view of the transcendental, there is nothing to suggest that he ever considered belief in God to be a relationship between a mind and an object. So if asked directly (by one of those students, perhaps) whether he believed in God, his response might have been, "I don't know—but if you mean what I think you mean, I really think not."

So there is a problem about whether Wittgenstein ever believed in God. But it is not basically a problem of finding this out about another person, idiosyncratic as his views may be. The basic problem is how one finds this out about oneself. If belief in God is a state of affairs in which a mind is related in a particular way to a particular entity, then the question whether one believes in God cannot be answered unless one knows what entity the term 'God' designates. But what 'God' designates is one of the most unsettled issued in the history of thought. So the ordinary person's response to the question whether he believes in God ought to be—like Wittgenstein's—"I really don't know." But this is not the ordinary response at all, since most people seem quite sure whether they are believers or not. If most people don't know what 'God' designates, how is this possible?

One reason some people tend to respond so readily to the question, "Do you believe in God?" may be that they take it to be equivalent to the question whether they accept the teachings of a particular religious group. If Group A teaches that God is (among other things) the sole creator of the universe, and if such a person accepts the teachings of Group A, then that person not only will affirm his or her belief in God but if asked what 'God' designates will reply (among other things), "the sole creator of the universe." But another person might accept the teachings of Group B, which teaches that God (among other things) existed coeternally with an uncreated universe. When this other person is asked about his belief in God, the answer will be, Yes, he believes in God, and that 'God' designates an entity coeternal with the universe. Both persons say they believe in God. But if there is something that created the universe, there is nothing with which the universe can be coeternal. Thus not both persons exist in a relationship with an entity that the term 'God' designates. Assuming that belief in God is a relationship with a particular entity, not both persons believe in God. Thus belief in God is not a matter merely of accepting the teachings of a religious group, regardless of what 'God' designates in the context of those teachings.

Suppose, however, that Group A is right in everything it teaches about God, and that the teachings of other groups are wrong in cases of conflict. Someone who accepts the teachings of Group A under these circumstances will have an answer to the question what the term 'God' designates, and may plausibly say that to believe in God is to accept these teachings. But this supposition of accuracy does not solve our present problem, which is to explain how a person can know whether he or she believes in God. Granted that one can know whether one accepts the teaching of a given religious tradition, it is quite another matter to find out whether those teachings are right. Even if the teachings of Group A include the "metateaching" that all Group A's teachings are accurate, that "metateaching" may be as erroneous as the teachings it endorses. Again we must conclude that acceptance of a set of teachings is not in itself to believe in God.

Another possible answer deals with proofs and reasons, as distinct from faith in a set of teachings. Suppose a person has encountered a rational argument (of his own, or another's devising) the bottom line of which is "therefore, God exists," and is convinced that the argument is correct and sound. We may assume as unproblematic that the person knows he accepts the argument, and even assume for sake of discussion that the argument is sound. Does it not follow that the person in this case knows whether or not he believes in God? The answer is "no." On the basis of the proof, the person believes that God exists. But believing that an entity exists bears no entailment relationship with believing in that entity. Believing that and beliving in are distinct states of mind. One could believe that capitalism exists in America without thereby believing in that institution, or believe there is a decision procedure for the first order predicate calculus without in any sense believing in that procedure. On the other hand, one might believe in civil rights or in complete forgiveness without in either case believing that the thing exists. Unlikely as it may be with any given individual, one could believe that God exists without believing in God (such a one, for instance, might be the devil); and one could even believe in God without believ-

112 A Perceptual Model of Belief in God

ing that God exists (a strict empiricist who restricted the term 'exists' to sensible things might nonetheless believe in God).

But perhaps the important point is not the distinction between these two kinds of believing. What is important, it might be suggested, is that reasons for believing that God exists might also be reasons for believing in God. Consider the case of a proof purportedly demonstrating the existence of a first efficient cause. In this case, reasons for believing that God exists will have something to do with the principle that all effects have causes and with the impossibility of an infinite regress. But these are not reasons for believing in God. Reasons for believing in God are, for example, that he has revealed himself in holy scripture, or that one has felt one's sins are forgiven. In response to the question why one believes in God, it would be inappropriate to respond "because all effects have causes," or "because all moving things are moved by others." The difference is not a matter merely of different examples; it is a matter rather of different kinds of reasons. Reasons for believing that such-and-such are reasons why something is the case, while reasons for believing in a thing are reasons for recognizing or accepting that thing. As the example of American capitalism illustrates, reasons why something is the case are not reasons for accepting it.

There is a more basic reason why reference to logical demonstrations will not explain how a given person can tell whether he or she believes in God. Consider the hypothetical case of the logician Thomas, who bears no particular resemblance to St. Thomas Aquinas except for having generated five proofs for the existence of God. The first proof concludes that necessarily there must exist a first mover, which (Thomas says incautiously) everyone understands to be God. The second concludes that necessarily there must be a first efficient cause, the third a necessary being, the fourth a cause of all perfection, and the fifth an intelligent governor directing all things to their end. In each case, the proof is followed by Thomas's assertion that the entity proved is what all men call God.

Now even if Thomas is right in this series of very general claims about our religious vocabulary, his proofs of God may be in trouble. That is, even though all mankind were to agree in giving the name 'God' to the first mover, the first efficient cause, and so forth, and even though the entities in question actually exist, it may be that we all are wrong in identifying God with these entities. Since in fact there is no general agreement in this regard, the difficulty only seems to be accentuated. Suppose one group of believers think of God as first mover, but not intelligent governor (Malebranche might be an example), and another as necessary being but not first mover (possibly St. Anselm belongs here), and so forth and so on for other combinations of characteristics. Then, although persons in each group all think of themselves as believing in God, some in fact are wrong in so thinking. Since God cannot be both first mover and not intelligent governor on the one hand, and necessary being but not first mover on the other, then the groups believing in entities under these two descriptions thereby cannot both believe in God. Although persons in both groups *think* they believe in God, at least one group believes in an entity which they mistakenly identify as God and hence do not believe in *God* at all. Analogously, a person might think he believes in capitalism, but think of capitalism as the economic system in which every individual has a right to equal monetary resources, in which case he does not believe in *capitalism*, but in something else wrongly called by that name.

The apparent upshot at this point is that unless a given person believes in God under a description that happens to be right, then despite what he or she thinks about the matter the person is simply wrong in thinking the belief is in God. So unless that person is an unusually competent and confident theologian (at least), he ought to respond

to the question whether he believes in God with a frank
and honest "I don't really know."

Now this is just the predicament in which we hypothet-
ically left Wittgenstein at the beginning of the discussion.
To arrive at the predicament, in either the particular or
the general case, we assumed (1) that 'God' unambigu-
ously designates a certain unique entity, and (2) that
'believing in' is a particular mental state in which the
believer assumes a certain attitude toward a particular
entity, from which it followed that 'believing in God' is a
determinate state of affairs that obtains or does not
obtain at a given time for a given person. Although these
assumptions might be challenged on other grounds as
well, what is wrong with them in this connection is just
that they lead to this unacceptable conclusion—that even
a reflective person cannot tell whether he believes in
God.

II

For a fresh start on our problem, let us try out yet
another interpretation of what we know about Wittgenstein's attitude toward religion. The background for this
interpretation—which we owe to Wittgenstein himself—
is the conception of religion as a form of life. To believe
in God, according to this conception, is not to entertain a
certain mental state in relationship to a certain unique
object. To believe in God rather is to engage in certain
exercises (e.g., going to church at regular intervals), to
participate in certain rituals (e.g., confession, communion), to be motivated by goals (e.g., salvation), and above
all, to observe certain proscriptions and prescriptions in
speaking of God. These practices and observances provide the context in which particular utterances about
God take on their uniquely religious meaning, and without which they cannot be properly understood at all. As
Wittgenstein said, to imagine a language is to imagine a

form of life.[1] Unless we understand the full context of personal involvement in which a given expression mentioning God is uttered, we cannot fully understand the expression itself. In particular, the expression "I believe in God" is part of a set of verbal rituals (e.g., the Credo), and takes on meaning for the believer in connection with those practices. Although the particular forms these practices take may vary among individuals, in this view such practices constitute belief in God.

When asked from a point of view outside religious practice, however, the question "Does so-and-so believe in God?" should be taken to mean the same as "Does so-and-so participate in such-and-such a language-game?" The application to Wittgenstein's own case is straightforward. Although he listed his religion as Roman Catholic because for the purpose of military records he had to take some stand on the matter, and although he spoke sympathetically of religion in conversation and writing, he did not (most of his life at least) participate actively in the practices and rituals that to his mind constitute religious belief; hence he did not believe in God.

Now I think this way of construing belief in God is preferable over the semantically rigid way of construing it as a mental relationship to a specific object. But there are some prominent features of the "form-of-life" construal that leave me basically dissatisfied. In raising these objections, I disclaim any pretense of knowing exactly how Wittgenstein thought of religion as a form of life. None of his writings are very explicit on this topic. My criticisms are against the "form-of-life" construal only as I understand it.

One problem with construing belief in God in terms of rituals and practices is that it appears to allow no distinction between right and wrong across a range of widely divergent religious beliefs. Criteria for distinguishing internally between true and false belief belong to the very bedrock on which a form of life is founded. But questions of correctness and incorrectness raised externally with regard to particular forms of life themselves, as it were, appear to lack a fulcrum to give them leverage. As Wittgenstein says in *On Certainty*, the form of life (world-picture) "is the substratum of all my enquiring and asserting," and if "the true is what is grounded, then the ground is not *true*, nor yet false" either.[2] The trouble with this, it seems to me, is that forms of life diverge so markedly across different religious beliefs that we cannot help feeling intuitively that not all are right. But if criteria of correctness are internal to individual forms of life as such, then whether given forms of life are correct or incorrect themselves cannot meaningfully be asked. The difficulty is not merely that we have no effective way of distinguishing correct from incorrect religious belief; it is that according to this view no such distinction seems even intelligible.

The major difficulty with this account identifying belief in God with participation in certain forms of life, however, is that the identity seems disproven both factually and conceptually. It is factually disproven, on the one hand, by participants in religious practices who in fact are not believers, and on the other hand by believers who do not participate in religious practices. It is conceptually disproven, in turn, by the very meaningfulness of such remarks as "It was because of his belief in God that he came finally to accept the rites of the Catholic Church," or "It was because of her long participation in Anglican rituals that she finally came to believe in God." Neither causal remark could constitute a genuine explanation if participation in religious practices of this sort were identical to belief in God.

If my argument to this point is sound, we have reasons for rejecting two extreme ways of thinking about man's belief in God. On one side is the referential model—the notion that the mind of the believer, as it were, casts a beam of intention into the realm of the eternal and unerringly spotlights the Divine Being itself. 'God' picks out God as 'Socrates' picks out Socrates, in this and any other possible world. What makes this feat we perform with 'God' doubly marvelous is that, unlike the case with the historical Socrates, we have no objective way of determining the features by which the Divine Being can be successfully spotlighted. On the other side is the "form-of-life" model—the theory according to which belief in God does not require any particular mental relationship with God at all. To believe in God is to engage in certain practices, which could be engaged in independently of whether God even exists. An adequate theory of religious belief, it seems to me, must find a middle ground between these two extremes.

III

In what follows I attempt to lay out an account of religious belief which avoids these difficulties of the "form-of-life" model. According to this account, belief in God is a certain manner of perceiving the world. Let us refer to this account as the "perceptual model."

Although there is no firm reason to think that Wittgenstein at any period of his life would have agreed with the perceptual model as I want to develop it, something closely akin is suggested in both the *Notebooks* and the *Tractatus*. Among Wittgenstein's numerous notebook entries on the 8th of July 1916, we find these two remarks: "To believe in God means to see that life has a meaning, and to believe in a God means to see that the facts of life are not the end of the matter." The term translated 'meaning' in the first mark is *Sinn*, which is generally used in the *Tractatus* to mean what a proposition represents in the domain of facts. There are two notable occurrences of the term in the *Tractatus*, however, where it takes on the less precise sense of "significance" or "value." One is at 6.41 in the remark that the "sense of the world must lie outside the world." The

other is in the parenthetical remark at 6.521, where
Wittgenstein is talking about the reason why "those who
have found after a long period of doubt that the sense of
life became clear to them have then been unable to say
what constituted that sense." It is in this latter sense of
Sinn, surely, that we are to understand—or at least try to
understand—how believing in God means seeing that
life has a meaning. To gloss the remark, we may read that
believing in God means to see that life has value or
significance, which from the companion remark we understand to have something to do with seeing that the
facts of life are not all there is to it.

Now I do not want to make much of a pair of remarks
which never found their way into the *Tractatus*, and the
exact meaning of which we have no way of discovering in
the first place. But there are two things Wittgenstein
seems to be saying in these remarks that I would like to
appropriate for my own use. For one, believing in God is
characterized as seeing things in a certain manner—
seeing that life has meaning, or seeing that the facts of
the world are not the end of the matter. Both terms in the
expression 'seeing that' require special comment. Although the term *sehen* here does not refer to visual
perception, it must have something to do with quality of
awareness. Presumably it means the same here as in the
penultimate sentence of the *Tractatus*, where Wittgenstein advises the reader that "He must transcend these
propositions, and then he will see the world aright." The
term 'that' in 'seeing that', moreover, does not indicate a
propositional object, at least in the sense of the *Tractatus*.
For there meaningful propositions pick out actual or
possible facts of the world, and that the facts of the world
are not the end of the matter is not another fact of the
world. In effect, to believe in God is to be aware of things
in a certain fashion, where the object of awareness is
neither factual nor propositional. To assure that awareness of this sort is intelligible is the main point behind

the *Tractatus*'s distinction between saying and showing (6.522).[3]

The second thing to note about the remarks quoted from the *Notebooks* is that the believer is characterized as viewing the world differently from the nonbeliever. The believer sees that the facts of the world are not all there is to it. The world is a different place for the believer, much as "The world of the happy man is a different one from that of the unhappy man" (6.43). In upshot, believing in God is not (or is not merely) maintaining some ethereal intentional relationship with an indiscernible object. It is rather to be aware of things that the unbeliever misses. To believe in God is to experience the world in some particular fashion.

In an effort to understand what this amounts to, let us break with Tractarian practice and consider some examples.

(Example 1): A. is a young and gifted violinist, for whom the frequent rehearsals of her college orchestra are the high point of a busy academic schedule. Once, during dress rehearsal for a Haydn Mass, which is going particularly well, A. becomes particularly attentive to the words of the chorus. She finds herself bowing out the message that the chorus is singing. As her response to the meaning intensifies, her awareness of sound yields to a sense of presence in which the music takes on the significance of the Mass itself. What is distinctive about this presence is not a particular object, but rather an immediate coalescense between subject and object. Self-awareness gives way to selfless unity. To experience the world in such a fashion is to believe in God.

(Example 2): B. is a homesteader in South Dakota, with two small children and an ailing wife. Cast of daylight and chill of night say the snows are coming, and only the animals keep the family warm in their summer lean-to. If B. and his family are to survive the winter, he must soon finish the house on which he is laboring feverishly. Because of crop failures during the summer, moreover, B. knows that somehow he must find some time for a trip to the trading post, to exchange one or two of his cows for flour and potatoes. Although tired and increasingly anxious as the days grow shorter, B. never yields to despair or panic. For whenever he pauses to reflect on the task before him, the sense takes form in his weary consciousness that help will come when he needs it most. For did not Jesus say "Look at the birds of the air: they neither sow nor reap nor gather into barns, and yet your heavenly Father feeds them." For B., God is a caring father, and to be mindful of that care is to believe in God.

(Example 3): C. is a social worker in a town near an Indian reservation in Arizona. Her husband is dead and her children grown. Several of her cases recently have involved people from the tribe who claim to have been injured under the influence of sorcery. C.'s own religion tells of demons and spirits, and she is convinced that she has spoken with her departed husband. Moreover, since beginning to deal with these Indian clients, she has several times caught sense of a malevolent presence which she could not dispel by accusing herself of superstition. Her dominant feeling on these occasions, nonetheless, was one of assurance, as if the spiritual forces of her religion were more than adequate protection. To feel protected against the unknown is to believe in God.

(Example 4): D. is a physical chemist, with a special interest in cosmology. Although fully convinced that scientific explanation of the elements cannot go further back than the "big bang" theory, D. finds that the concept of God somehow makes the universe more intelligible. When he reads in the Gospel that first there was Logos, this means to him that in the beginning was order. And since he understands order to be convertible with both information and energy, he thinks of creation as a transformation of order to energy, at which point the "big bang" inaugurates the physical universe. Thinking of God as principle of order also suggests an answer to the troublesome question, whence the structure in the first place that is constantly giving way to entropy? Such thoughts he insists are not scientific, but they are continuous with cosmology as a developing scientific theory. To find the universe intelligible beyond science is to believe in God.

Further examples of this sort could be developed to illustrate the responses of a believer to grief, guilt, injustice, mortality, temptation, and so forth. Let me instead make some generalizations based on the examples before us.

First, a series of qualifications. Although each of these examples involves the response of an individual to a particular set of circumstances (or with D., a particular type of situation), we do not think of an individual's belief as confined to particular responses. For B. to believe in God is not just for him to exhibit hope and trust in a situation of increasing stress. It is also for him to be prepared to act like this on similar occasions, and perhaps to act like A. or C. when his situation invites it. Like other forms of belief generally, belief in God is dispositional.

At the same time, belief in God is not merely a disposition to certain forms of behavior. One could act with hope and trust in dire situations for reasons that have no particular religious significance. Some people are intrepid in their self-reliance, while others don't get worried come what may. The dispositions typical of religious belief, rather, are bound up with certain ways of viewing human vicissitude. It is because B. looks upon hardship

as within the ken of a caring Father that he continues
work with confidence upon his family's shelter, and
because C. views psychic phenomena as in the domain of
an all-encompassing beneficence that she responds to
spiritual threat with equanimity. To believe in God is to
be disposed to certain forms of behavior, under the
perception of the world as a certain type of place.

Another qualification is that belief obviously is not
manifest only in a person's response to extraordinary
circumstances, although it may be in such circumstances
that belief is most evident. Belief can be manifest as well
in day-by-day living. For instance, A.'s persistence while
preparing for a difficult final examination could be due
to her viewing the preparation as an act of devotion.

A further general point is that in each of the examples,
belief in God was described without drawing upon any
special philosophical or theological vocabulary. There
was no mention of such theoretically arrived-at notions
as "first efficient cause," "prime mover," or "necessary
being," upon which specialists often rely in explicating
their conceptions of divinity. In fact, there was no mention of God under any particular referential description
at all. This is not to say that God drops out of this account
of religious belief, as seems to be the case under the
"form-of-life" model. It is to say rather that God's role in
this account does not depend upon his having any particular features beyond those made evident in the believer's personal experience. To believe in God is not
necessarily—and perhaps is seldom—to believe in an
object under a theoretical description.

The final thing I want to point out about the examples
is that in none of them does belief take the form of an
intentional attitude. A.'s mental attitude, if anything, is
one of unmediated rapture, while D.'s is a general readi-
ness to look beyond the confines of science. B.'s and C.'s
attitudes in turn are forms of assurance—a confidence in
the face of unsettling experience. Although someone
might be tempted to redescribe these situations in terms

of propositional attitudes ("C. believed that God would protect her," etc.), such an attempt would be gratuitous, because the beliefs in question are not propositional. The beliefs of B. and C. are not beliefs that certain facts are the case, but rather acceptance of certain facts in light of a certain way of viewing them. In upshot, belief in God in these examples is neither intentional in the sense of being directed upon a particular object nor intentional in the sense of involving a propositional attitude. Although there is no reason why belief on particular occasions might not have intentional components, belief in God does not seem typically to be an intentional attitude.

IV

This discussion began with a series of difficulties stemming from the referential model of religious belief, according to which 'God' in 'belief in God' refers to a unique entity that can be picked out in terms of specific characteristics, and 'belief' in that expression refers to a specific mental attitude with that entity as its intentional object. We turned next to a more promising way of conceiving religious belief, adopted from the thought of the later Wittgenstein. A major virtue of this "form-of-life" model is that it avoids the vices of the intentional model. Its main difficulty is that it seems to err in the opposite extreme, severing in effect all referential connections between religious practice and the object of worship. A consequence is that no distinction appears available between correct and incorrect religious belief. I wish now to draw upon the four examples to formulate an alternative to these two extremes.

In the context of these examples, belief in God is a capacity to respond in certain ways to certain experiences, under the perception of the world as a certain sort of place. B. is able to face the threat of approaching winter because he views the world as a place in which human needs make a difference. Although B. does not perceive God as he perceives the sun and the prairie, his perception of objects in the world is permeated by a sense of coherence in which human interests are integrated with the rest of nature. The remark that "The world and life are one," appearing in both the *Tractatus* (5.621) and the *Notebooks* (24.7.16), may convey this perception as part of its meaning. Likewise, when this mode of awareness is confronted with an experience of evil, it counters with a sense of indefeasible integrity. As C.'s encounter with sorcery illustrates, to paraphrase another remark of the early Wittgenstein, what is good is more harmonious than what is bad (*Notebooks* 30.7.16).

But it is the case of A. that best illustrates the integrated awareness that seems to be typical of belief in God. For when the meaning of the music converged with the meaning of the liturgy, A. became aware of a comprehensive unity, which—following the testimony of the mystics—we may call a form of divinity. In this awareness the distinction fades between self and object; the self shrinks, as Wittgenstein puts it (*Tractatus* 5.64), to an extensionless point. This means that the awareness becomes occupied with a selfless reality, which being "how things stand" is identical with God (*Notebooks* 1.8.16).

To believe in God is to see the world in a certain manner. When near despair, it is to perceive a world where human needs make a difference. When afflicted with injustice, it is to see a world in which righteousness prevails. When mournful, it is to see the world as offering comfort; when moved to mercy, to see an order in which mercy is rewarded. The beatitudes are formulae shaping the world of the believer. In enjoining them Jesus enjoined belief in God.

According to the perceptual model, in brief and in sum, to believe in God is to view the world as possessing a comprehensive significance in which human vicissitudes are ultimately meaningful. By 'comprehensive significance' here, I mean an all-compassing order in which human experience fits with the rest of nature. And by suggesting that human vicissitude in this order is ultimately meaningful, I mean that the unaccountable excursions of human experience finally cease to appear gratuitous. This is what I take Wittgenstein to have meant when he said, succinctly, that to believe in God is to see that life has a meaning (*Notebooks* 8.7.16).

It would be presumptuous to suggest that this perceptual model somehow captures the "essence" of religious belief. My suspicion is that religious belief has no "essence" to capture. Behind the objections to the referential model developed at the beginning of this discussion is a sense that this model responds to a conception of belief in God according to which such belief always occurs with a certain fixed nature—in this case, as a specific mental relationship with a specific entity. I think this is a mistake quite apart from the particular way this alleged nature is construed by the referential model. For this reason also, I think it would be a mistake to attempt any definitive characterization of how one must view the world if one's way of viewing the world is to count as belief in God. Various ways can be ruled out, of course, such as viewing the world as meaningless, or as irredeemably evil. Clear cases of belief, on the other hand, are the ways of seeing things enjoined by the beatitudes. But I believe there is no border between these extremes where belief and nonbelief can be clearly distinguished. The only claim in behalf of the perceptual model with which I really feel comfortable is the following. It represents more closely than either the referential or the "form-of-life" models what it is among persons I have known intimately that distinguishes those who believe in God.

Nonetheless, I believe the perceptual model can be recommended on philosophic grounds. Whereas the main advantage of the "form-of-life" model mentioned above is that it avoids the difficulties of the referential model, the main advantage of the perceptual model in turn may be that it can avoid the difficulties of the "form-of-life" model.

One problem of the "form-of-life" model as I understand it is that it allows no intelligible distinction between correct and incorrect religious belief. According to the perceptual model, on the other hand, a person who believes in God (perceives the world as having a certain significance) has a correct belief (perceives the world correctly) if and only if the world in fact possesses significance of that sort. Analogously, a person who perceives the world as structured by objects in space and time (believes the world is so structured) perceives the world correctly (has a correct belief) if and only if the world in fact has that structure. Problems of considerable philosophic difficulty remain in attempting to specify the structure of perceptual objects; but if objects are not structured the way we perceive them then there is a sense in which our perception is incorrect. Similarly, although considerable problems remain in specifying the ultimate significance of the world we experience, there is a sense in which a person who perceives the world as having a certain form of significance would perceive incorrectly if nothing existed in the world corresponding to that perception. Whatever correct belief might amount to, at very least the distinction between correct and incorrect religious belief is intelligible in the context of the perceptual model.

The main problem of the "form-of-life" model of belief in God is that there seems to be no incongruity in saying of a given person either that he engages in religious practice but is not a believer, or that he believes in God but does not engage in religious practice. What this indicates is that belief in God is not primarily a certain form of behavior. On the other hand, there does appear to be something incongruous about the notion of a believer in God who views the world as meaningless and foreign to human existence, or about the notion of a person who views the world as in the domain of an all-compassing beneficence (as with C. above, for example) but does not at the same time believe in God. What this indicates is that belief in God has something directly to do with how one views the world.

As an epilogue, consider once more whether Wittgenstein believed in God. Since this perceptual account of belief has been illustrated by remarks from the *Notebooks* and the *Tractatus*, it appears that Wittgenstein at least understood the question about the meaning of life. And to understand this, he said in the *Notebooks* (8.7.16), is to believe in God.

NOTES

1. *Philosophical Investigations*, trans. G. E. M. Anscombe (Oxford: Blackwell, 1953), p. 19.

2. *On Certainty* (New York: Harper and Row, 1969), pp. 162, 205.

3. *Tractatus Logico-Philosophicus* (London: Routledge and Kegan Paul, 1961). See the letter to Ficher quoted in A. Janik and S. Toulmin *Wittgenstein's Vienna* (New York: Simon and Schuster, 1973), p. 192.

The Christian Language-Game

WILLIAM P. ALSTON

I

It is obvious that involvement in a religion *is* a "form of life" in a natural sense of the term. Moreover this is not just one partial section of life among others; it imposes a certain form on the whole of one's life. To the extent that one is committed to, e.g., Christianity, one will see one's personal relationships, duties, work, afflictions, and so on, in a distinctive way. Attitudes towards other people, social problems, and the course of history will be affected. One will react differently to success and failure, to professional opportunities, to the behavior of associates. Priorities will be different from what they would be otherwise. Furthermore there will be a certain integration and unification of all one's attitudes and activities under the aegis of the central foci of the religion. All this is very salient to a person who moves in and out of religious involvement.

I advert to these well-worn platitudes only to set them aside. My use of the correlated Wittgensteinian notions of *form of life* and *language-game* will go beyond the familiar points just mentioned, though not in a way unconnected from them. Like most ideas in the later Wittgenstein, the notions of *form of life* and *language-game* admit of a variety of applications and elaborations, not all of them mutually compatible. I shall have to extricate my use of these terms from the dense and rather chaotic web of the *Philosophical Investigations*. To avoid bogging down in a mire of Wittgensteinian exegesis, I shall mention only those aspects of Wittgenstein's discussion that are specially relevant to highlighting my use of the terms.

Let's begin with the point that a language-game is a more or less distinctive and more or less unified *practice* of using language. The term 'form of life' is thrown in to emphasize the point that a practice of using language is integrally connected with nonlinguistic activities. (In this paper I will use 'language-game' rather than 'form of life' as being less ill-suited to the concept with which I shall be working.) However, this characterization leaves open a great many alternatives. To what extent, and in what ways, does a practice have to be distinctive and unified in order to count as a distinct language-game? We seem to have conflicting principles of individuation at work in the *Philosophical Investigations*. Sometimes the suggestion is that different illocutionary forces will constitute different language-games. Thus in #23 examples of lan-guage-games include such items as

> Giving orders, and obeying them —
> Describing the appearance of an object . . .
> Reporting an event —
> Speculating about an event —
> Forming and testing a hypothesis —
> Asking, thanking, cursing, greeting, praying.

The earlier sections with the "primitive" language-games of giving orders and giving reports point in the same direction. Sometimes "content" restrictions are added to illocutionary force, as when Wittgenstein speaks of confessing motives, color-ascriptions, or "I meant this," as contrasted with "I thought of this as I said it," as a language-game. He even suggests in one place that whatever we do with a given *word*, in this case 'game', counts as a distinct language-game (pp. 24–25, 217, 34).

I infer from all this that Wittgenstein was not seriously concerned to use the term 'language-game' with any

single consistent criterion of individuation, but was
rather concerned to exploit the point that any type of
speech act forms part of a learned practice that involves
nonlinguistic as well as linguistic aspects and that understanding some of the details of this in particular cases
enables us to make a proper response to the philosophical problems that are raised about various spheres of
discourse.

In any event, it is in that spirit that I shall apply the
term 'language-game' in this paper. My way of dividing
up discourse into distinct language-games is dictated by
an interest in throwing light on the interpretation and on
the epistemic status of religious belief, more specifically
beliefs about God in the Judaeo-Christian tradition, and,
still more specifically, Christian belief about God. Hence
I will be exploring the possibility that Christian discourse
constitutes a distinctive language-game in such a way as
to carry distinctive implications for the understanding of
concepts and the rationality of belief. A language-game,
on this mode of individuation, will be distinguished in
terms of "subject-matter"—physical objects, persons,
mathematical entities, etc.; and each language-game will
include a large range of illocutionary-act types (stating,
predicting, hypothesizing, expressing feelings and attitudes, conjecturing, remarking), though not every
illocutionary-act type will be possible in every language-
game. For example, promising, thanking, and confessing are only suitable for games concerned with "personal" beings. The language-games to be considered in
this paper will all involve illocutionary acts of the asser-
tive type—truth claims—together with such other
illocutionary-act types as are appropriate to the subject
matter. Though Wittgenstein was not given to applying
the term 'language-game' to units like this, I would
suppose that, in effect, he was treating talk about feelings
and sensations, for example (and perhaps other modes
of experience as well), as a distinctive language-game.

The games I shall be considering are those "dealing" with (1) conscious experience, (2) the physical world, (3) human persons, and (4) God.

II

What makes a certain language-game distinct from others? And what makes it a single language-game rather than an aggregate of two or more? I can't go into these questions with the fullness they deserve. But the following kinds of considerations would be crucial to an adequate answer.

The Ontology

Each language-game defines a type (or types) of entity, defined by "categoreal" characteristics. Thus the (common sense) "physical-world language-game" features at least two basic types of entities—physical things and physical stuff. Physical things are defined by such categoreal features as (a) being relatively stable and relatively permanent substances that retain their self-identity through change, (b) possessing size, shape, and such physical properties as mass, temperature, and the like, and (c) being distributed in space. (I will abstain from giving the categoreal characteristics of physical stuff.)

Categoreal types of entities come equipped with modes of identification, reidentification, and individuation. There are standard procedures for answering questions as to how to pick out a particular book, how many books there are on the shelf, and whether the book on the end of the second row is the same one as the book that was there this time yesterday.

Similarly the "human-person language-game" ranges over a categoreal type defined by such features as (a) being a living body of a certain sort, (b) carrying out cognitive and conative activities, and (c) performing intentional purposive actions. Procedures of identification, reidentification, and individuation are also involved.

The Ideology (to borrow a useful term from Quine)

This is the "conceptual scheme," as contrasted with the range(s) of individuals to which the concepts may be applied. The basic idea is that there are certain kinds of concepts that *can* be applied to, e.g., physical objects or to human persons, and other kinds that cannot. For example, it is a live question whether a certain person is thinking about the weather, but not whether a certain stone or a certain sense-datum is doing so. And, to take a well-worn example, we can wonder what the back of that house looks like but not what the back of this sense-datum (or the back of a number or of a Euclidean triangle) looks like. It would be nice to be able to exhibit a certain conceptual scheme as a tightly integrated system, with relatively few determinables under which all the concepts of the system fall as determinates, or as a few basic concepts on the basis of which all the concepts in the scheme can be defined. But whether or not this is possible, presumably something can be done to indicate what does and does not fall within the scheme, and the patterns of implication and exclusion can be indicated to some extent.

It may not be obvious, in the abstract, where to draw the line between the categoreal features that define a type of individual, and the further sorts of concepts that can be applied to entities of that type; and in practice there may be plenty of borderline cases. But there are many clear cases as well. It seems clear that spatial position is part of what makes something a physical object, while crystalline structure is merely something it makes sense to attribute to it. In any possible world physical objects will have spatial position, while in some possible worlds none of them will have crystalline structure.

The Epistemology

Another crucial respect in which a language-game is distinct is that the justification (rationality) of assertions (beliefs, judgments) in that game does not depend (at least does not essentially depend) on support from what is known or justifiably believed in other language-games. Each language-game enjoys what we may call epistemic autonomy. For the range of language-games we are considering in this paper, this may be further spelled out as follows. An essential part of what one learns in learning a particular language-game is how to make (justified, approved) "immediate" applications of some of the terms of that game, on the basis of experience. The force of calling these applications "immediate" is that they are not justified by inference, or any other sort of derivation, from other things the subject knows or justifiably believes. These applications are on the basis of experience, not in the sense that they are inferred from statements about the character of one's experience at the moment, but in the sense that they are applied on the occasion of experience. The "player" has acquired the ability to react differentially to different "cues" in his experience, without thereby taking those cues as themselves objects of knowledge or belief from which the applications in question are inferred. Thus to say that the physical-world language-game is epistemically autonomous in this way is to claim that perceptual judgments about physical objects, though made on the occasion of sensory experience, do not need to be inferrable from (true, known) statements about the character of that experience in order to be justifiably or rationally held. What makes a particular physical-object perceptual belief *rational* is that it was formed as part of a (learned) practice that is in fact reliable. Similarly, when I see that my wife is angry, or relieved, or thinking hard about something, what I come to believe about her does not have to be inferrable from "physical" facts about bodily movements or position in

order that I be justified in these beliefs. We may sum this
up by saying that in these language-games there is an
established practice of immediately applying terms on
the basis of experience.

Epistemic autonomy also involves a distinctive mode of
supporting other beliefs on the basis of reasons. What
makes a reason a good reason is different for talk about
physical objects, about a person's motives, and so on.*

With respect to the relations between language-games,
the distinctive features we have mentioned are man-
ifested in a certain independence and irreducibility.
Conceptually, the concepts of a language-game form a
"closed circle"; although interdefinition may be possible
to various degrees within a language-game, there is no
possibility of defining all, or some, of the concepts of a
given language-game on the basis of "outside" concepts.
The history of philosophy is littered with unsuccessful
attempts to do just this—exhibit physical object terms as
constructs out of phenomenal terms, P-predicates as
definable physicalistically, action concepts as built up out
of causal concepts, ethical concepts as definable
psychologically, and so on. Ontologically, the entities of a
language-game are deployed in a "space" that is completely filled with the native population; there is no room
for outsiders. Thus sense-data cannot be fitted into physical space, there is no room in the body for the mind,
agency does not fit into the interstices of causal interaction, and so on. Epistemologically, the numerous attempts to "prove" the existence of the external world on
the basis of one's own private sensory experience, or to
prove the existence of other minds on the basis of pub-
licly observable physical facts, have failed to carry conviction.

*There may be other important distinguishing features of language-games
of the sorts under consideration here, e.g., the "logic." But for present
purposes we will restrict ourselves to the features listed above.

In fact, irreducibility and autonomy serve as crucial indicators of distinctness of language-games or, to put it another way, the justification for positing a separate language-game will depend on the outcome of controversies over reducibility and autonomy. From a phenomenalist position physical-object talk does not constitute a separate language-game, and for certain kinds of positivism there is no diversity of language-games in the sense envisaged in this paper.

Two considerations blur somewhat the sharp outlines we have been drawing up to now. First, the autonomy of language-games is not absolute, and different cases differ in degree of autonomy. Facts about sensory experience can be used as evidence for physical-object statements ("It looks like a cow, doesn't it?"). Since it is plausible to regard "If it looks red in normal circumstances it is red" as a conceptual truth it is correspondingly possible to think of the physical-object predicate 'red' as being partly definable on the basis of the phenomenal predicate 'red'. And human persons have (or are) bodies that qualify as clear cases of physical objects. But despite these partial dependencies, there is no complete reduction or dependence in these cases. Its looking like a cow counts as evidence for its being a cow only in the context of physical-object assumptions about the conditions of that perception. And in the second example a physical object's *being red* can be defined as its *looking red* only with the addition of the further physical world qualification 'in normal circumstances'. Finally, if a human person is a physical object, it is also something else of a different category; at least this is being supposed by anyone who thinks of the human-person language-game as a distinct game. Thus we can say that a distinct language-game will enjoy a significant degree of autonomy in the respects specified. Of course, since it is a matter of degree there can be no precise answer to the question "How much autonomy is sufficient?" But that does not prevent us from identifying cases where the degree of autonomy exemplified is of considerable philosophical importance.

Second, it is possible for a sphere of discourse to be autonomous in some respects and not others. Let's say that terms for colors, shapes, and various other properties of physical objects cannot be defined in terms of other physical-object terms. Color terms, shape terms, etc., each constitute an irreducible sphere of concepts. Furthermore there are immediate applications of color terms, of shape terms, and so on. On the other hand, these terms all apply to entities of the same category; there is no ontological autonomy. Hence we do not think of them as constituting distinct language-games. Again, theoretical terms in science may not be definable solely by the use of observational terms; and if that is so, it would seem that theoretical statements cannot be justified wholly by observation statements (empirical confirmation is always in the context of other theoretical principles). Even so the theoretical entities *may* be of the same categoreal type as observable physical objects. For present purposes, let's rule that a distinct language-game has to exhibit a significant degree of autonomy in all the respects we have mentioned. This will prevent the "Balkanization" of language-games into minute components that are autonomous in some respects but not others.

Wittgenstein was especially concerned to make the point that a language-game is a learned practice; more specifically, he stressed the point that we learn to do it not be being taught the theory of it or by having rules formulated for us, but by imitation, being corrected when we go wrong, and so on. I don't think it is necessary to state this point in terms of any specific claims about the psychology of learning. The essential philosophical point is that by the time we reach the stage of philosophical reflection we *find* ourselves engaged in these practices, we *find* that we have thoroughly mastered them. But despite this mastery and this entrenchment, we do not find ourselves in possession of explicitly formulated criteria for the application of concepts, for the justification of assertions, much less for the demarcation of ontological types.

Another crucial feature of the Wittgensteinian notion is that a language-game is not just something we do with *words*—like anagrams or Swifties—but that learning a language-game essentially involves learning how to act and react to the entities we are learning to conceptually structure in a certain way in that language-game. Learning the physical-object game is not just a matter of learning the logical relations between concepts, etc., but it is also a matter of learning both to recognize instances of a concept in the environment *and also* how to act toward those instances in the pursuit of various goals. Similarly, learning the human-person game is not just learning the conceptual scheme, but it is also learning how to treat something *as* a person, and, indeed, what it is to *be* a person. From some philosophical perspectives, there is a sharp separation between cognitive learning and practical skills, but the Wittgensteinian language-game scheme embodies a quite different approach. From this perspective one can't understand our concept of a physical object, or of a person, without understanding what it is to take appropriate account of physical objects or of persons in our environment.

I am all too keenly aware of the fragmentary and superficial character of the foregoing exposition. I have given only a few (putative) examples of the basic concepts like categoreal type and immediate application. I have been forced to issue *obiter dicta* on many highly controversial points. My aspiration has merely been to give some sense of a certain way of looking at these areas of discourse as (relatively) autonomous language-games, as a background for raising the question as to whether Christian discourse can be viewed as one or more language-games of this ilk.

Sprachspiel afficionados will have been struck by certain

signal omissions from my list of distinguishing features. I have not echoed the familiar claims that each distinct language-game embodies distinctive concepts of truth and reality. The omission was deliberate. My quarrel with Phillips, Winch, and (perhaps) Wittgenstein on this point reflects philosophical differences at a very deep level. I am an unreconstructed realist who is committed to the view that truth is independent of epistemic considerations, of what is recognized in one or another language-game as constituting justification, rationality, or acceptability. What it takes to make a proposition true is uniquely determined by the content of the proposition, what it "says." If what we are saying is that snow is white, to coin a phrase, then what it takes to make the proposition true is simply that snow *be* white. Of course *what* is said by assertions in different language-games will be importantly different, because we will be referring and generalizing over different ranges of entities, and applying different concepts to them. (And hence what is required to be justified in an assertion will be correspondingly different.) But a common formula, spanning language-game differences, can be given for what makes any assertion true, viz., that what is being talked about in the assertion *is* as the assertion says it is. The idea that there is something wrong with this common-sense notion of truth stems, I believe, entirely from verificationist ways of thinking that should be thoroughly exploded by now but still exert a profound influence on the contemporary philosophical scene, all the more profound for being, usually, unacknowledged. Nor is the support for this realist view limited to pointing out that it is a powerfully appealing common-sense notion that cannot be refuted. I believe there to be no coherent alternative to the idea that our thought and discourse essentially presupposes common concepts of reference and truth that range over all (statemental) discourse. Unfortunately I cannot go further into this matter in this paper.

III

With this background we can turn to our central question—can Christian discourse be construed as constituting a language-game that is distinct conceptually, ontologically, and epistemically? Or rather, remembering that autonomy is a matter of degree, to what extent does Christian discourse fit our requirements for language-game distinctness? This is a question of the utmost importance for the philosophy of religion, since it profoundly affects the interpretation of theological concepts, our conception of the nature and reality of God, and the kind of support Christian belief needs in order to be rational.

Let me present the case for the language-game distinctness of Christian discourse in the three basic respects presented above.

The distinctive ontological commitment of Christian discourse (if we omit angels and other relatively inessential paraphernalia) is to a single being, God. The issue of distinctness of ontological framework *is* the question of whether God can be construed as an example of some type of entity figuring in some other language-game. The case for denying this can be made in various ways, and these ways differ along various dimensions. They differ in terms of how "objective" they take the reality of God to be, ranging from what I would term more subjective views, like that of Phillips and Randall, to the more objective conceptions that we find in Augustine, Anselm, Aquinas, and other theologians in the mainstream of Christian thought. As my previous remarks on truth might indicate, I shall align myself with the latter group. From this standpoint, we have a wealth of divine attributes that sharply distinguish God from all other entities and that could plausibly be taken as categoreal features. For example: (1) God is being-itself; (2) God is infinite being, containing the full richness of being, and hence cannot be confined to any particular species; (3) God exists necessarily. There are, of course, different ways of taking one or more of these features as basic categoreal features and deriving the others from that base. The general point is that if we follow the classic tradition in stressing the uniqueness of God in these or other respects, and oppose the "anthropomorphizing" tendency to regard God as simply a bigger, more perfect, more powerful person, then talk about God involves a distinct ontology.*

The claim that Christian discourse involves a distinct and irreducible *conceptual scheme* may seem to conflict with the well-advertised fact that theological terms are taken from our talk of creatures. But though this is, in the main, undeniable, it is almost as widely accepted that these terms, or most of them, cannot be used of God and creatures in the same senses. The categoreal features that make God a distinct sort of entity would seem to militate against univocal predication. How could an infinite, necessary being that *is* being itself *make*, *cause*, *speak*, *love*, or *forgive* in the senses of those terms in which they are applicable to human beings? I myself feel that the prohibition on univocal predication has been leveled in too undiscriminating a fashion. I have argued elsewhere that if we make our terms that apply to human beings abstract and unspecific enough they could con-

---

*Of course, Christian discourse is not just about God, but also about human beings, the world of nature, inner experience, and so on. Nevertheless the creation comes into the picture only *as* God's creation and *as* related to God in other ways. Thus God is the basic entity for this discourse. To what extent is Christian discourse unlike other language-games in ranging over entities of all ontological types, from a certain perspective? Well, it appears that language-games differ in this regard. Large stretches of our discourse range over entities of a single type. We can envisage the possibility of a totally self-enclosed physical-object discourse that never mentions relations to other sorts of things whereas language-games that have to do centrally with purposive agents, whether human, divine, or otherwise, cannot be concerned just with purposive agents, for it is essential to, or at least typical of, agents, that their purposes extend to things that are not of their own kind.

ceivably apply in the same sense to God. But even if that is so, the fact remains that when we are dealing with concepts at a more specific level, the level at which we are actually working in most first-level religious discourse, we cannot fail to recognize that what it is for God to speak, love, forgive, or make must be radically different from what it is for human beings to do those things. And so insofar as our concepts embody that distinctiveness they will be significantly different from the concepts we apply to human persons. Of course that in itself does not show that these concepts are irreducible to concepts applying to creatures, but I am unaware of any promising attempts to carry out such a reduction, at least among thinkers who fully recognize God's categoreal uniqueness.

How is the Christian conceptual scheme to be acquired if it cannot be explained on the basis of conceptual schemes that apply to creatures? This question forces us to make explicit a hitherto unmentioned feature of the language-game approach to these matters. To my mind, one of Wittgenstein's most valuable insights is that the basic terms of a language-game are acquired in the course of learning a practice, where, as indicated earlier, this practice involves nonlinguistic as well as linguistic elements. We do not acquire the physical-object vocabulary from definitions constituted on a phenomenal base. Nor do we learn it by "ostensive definition," i.e., by having various types of physical objects and exemplifications of various physical-object properties pointed out to us while the appropriate word is being enunciated. It can't be this way, as Wilfrid Sellars has pointed out so clearly, just because we can't "pick out" or "notice" the physical object or property exemplification in question until we have the conceptual resources to do so, i.e., until we have already learned terms of the sort in question. That sort of learning presupposes the prior possession of what is to be learned. It is rather that in being trained to react appropriately to physical objects, in the light of their nature, conditions, and distribution in space, we acquire the concepts, the terminology, and the practical skills all at once, as a complete package. There is no way in which we could acquire a part of this package without the rest.

In treating Christian discourse along the lines of this model, we are taking it that the same kind of story is to be given of the acquisition of the Christian conceptual framework. The details will be enormously different. Apart from all other differences it seems that the physical-object conceptual framework can be the first one learned, whereas, whatever the logical possibilities, the theological framework is learned on the basis of prior abilities to talk about human persons and the physical world. But in both cases we will think of the concepts being acquired in the course of learning to react appropriately to the distinctive entities of that language-game; we can't have the basic distinctive concepts of that sphere of discourse without knowing how to use them in the guidance of conduct. Applied to the Christian case, this means that one learns what it is for God to be merciful, loving, and gracious in the course of learning, e.g., to see one's existence and the world around one as a gift of God, and learning to respond to this with thankfulness. One learns what it means for the Holy Spirit to be within us by learning to recognize certain incidents in life as consisting in the guidance or strengthening of one by the Holy Spirit, and to take this as authoritative and meaningful in a certain way.

In its references to, e.g., seeing various things as gifts of God, the last paragraph hints at the third distinctive feature of language-games, epistemic autonomy. Remember that the crucial requirement for epistemic autonomy (in statemental language-games dealing with concrete rather than abstract objects) is that there be an established practice of immediate applications of terms on the basis of experience, applications justified just by being made on the appropriate occasion of experience, rather than by the possession of adequate reasons in the shape of something else the person knows. Is this crucial requirement satisfied for the Christian language-game?

The case for supposing that it is met would be that "training in Christianity" essentially involves learning to see various things, in the world and in one's life and experience, as manifestations of God. One learns to see the beauty of the world as a gift of God; one learns to see good and ill fortune as blessings of God or as trials sent by God to test us or to provide the occasion for moral and spiritual growth. One prays for courage to face a difficult situation or for guidance in making a difficult decision; and when one faces the situation courageously or sees the way to making the decision (if one does) one takes this as guidance or illumination by God (the Holy Spirit). One learns to take the bread and wine of the Eucharist (I'm trying to steer clear of doctrinal controversies here as much as possible) as a communion with Christ and as a reception of the indwelling spirit of Christ. One learns to hear God speaking to one in the Bible, in preaching, or in more informal encounters with other persons. If, at a certain point, one finds oneself in possession of a new ability to love the people around one, including those one tends to find not so lovable, one will see this as the Holy Spirit working within one.

In all these cases, we have what might be called "mediated immediacy"; these are all cases of coming to see X as Y. That is, we already had learned to recognize the situation as involving an X; now we learn to take it as a Y also. The immediacy involved is epistemic; that is, we don't take it as a Y because we think we have adequate reasons for doing so; we just experience it that way.* Here the relation of the Christian and the natural-world

---

*Here my version of Sprachspielism is greatly indebted to John Hick, who does not present his views in the language-game format. See his *Faith and Knowledge*, 2nd ed. (Ithaca, N.Y.: Cornell University Press, 1966), pts. II and III.

language-games is rather analogous to that between the physical-world and human-person games. In the latter case, ignoring the issue of genetic development, it is obvious that our perception of other persons as persons is mediated through our perception of their bodies as physical objects. We don't learn to conceptualize our (otherwise unstructured) *experience* in terms of personalistic categories. We learn to see physical objects (recognized as such) as personal agents, doing, feeling, and thinking various things, though, on the view being presupposed here, we don't rest our most basic beliefs about other persons on physical facts about their bodies.

One may also wonder whether any more purely immediate experience of God plays any role in the Christian language-game. Looking at the models from which we are working we can discern two further grades of immediacy. The conscious-experience game embodies the purest sort of immediacy. We are in *no* way experiencing feelings, sensations, or thoughts *through* something else of a different categoreal type; we are in no sense seeing X *as* a feeling, where X is something that we are prepared to conceptualize within some other language-game. Nor is there any need to support beliefs about one's own current conscious experience with reasons drawn from knowledge of a different sphere of reality. The physical-world game is intermediate in these respects. Genetically, it is plausible to suppose that we learn physical-world talk before learning conscious-experience talk. And, apart from that, it seems that my capacity to pick out and describe objects in the environment on the basis of experience is independent of my ability to talk about experience as private modifications of myself. This is indicated by, e.g., the well-known fact that the discriminations we make within sensory experience are made in terms drawn from our talk of physical objects. But despite this, there are well-known philosophical moves that seem to force us to recognize that our knowledge of our own states of consciousness is more direct than our perceptual knowledge of physical objects, and that, in some sense, we get at the latter through the former. Furthermore in some cases we do support perceptual judgments about physical objects by facts about our sensory experience ("It must be a car; otherwise it wouldn't have that shiny appearance"), and the full development of physical-object talk involves the ability to pop back and forth between it and phenomenal talk—judging the real color of an object by how it looks in different lighting, etc. Thus we may distinguish three grades of immediacy.

1. Absolute immediacy (phenomenal language-game)—in no sense are the basic statements epistemically grounded on others, nor are the objects in any sense experienced *through* other objects.

2. Intermediate immediacy (physical-world language-game)—the basic statements can be made without the mastery of the phenomenal language-game, statements of which can be, and sometimes are, taken as reasons. In some sense, physical objects are experienced through sensory impressions, though normally it is not a case of sensory impressions being seen *as* physical objects.

3. Mediated immediacy (human-person language-game)—normally the mastery of this language-game is based on (or at least acquired along with) mastery of the physical-world game. (It is not clear whether the person game could be acquired without reliance on the physical-world game.) This goes along with the fact that normally we would know how to give physical-object statements in support of at least some person statements (particularly action statements), though, of course, in regarding this as a distinct language-game, we are regarding the most basic person statements as not resting wholly on statements from a different language-game. Fur-

thermore, the experience of a human person is appropriately described as seeing a physical object of a certain kind *as* a person.

I have already illustrated mediate immediacy. What about the other two? Epistemological discussions of religious experience have — unfortunately, in my opinion — concentrated on mystical experience. Presumably this is partly because of its striking character and partly because, despite its putative ineffability, it is easily demarcated from other modes of experience. Furthermore it has generally been treated as exemplifying pure immediacy, indeed an even more absolute immediacy than our experience of our own feelings and sensations, since one of the distinguishing features of mystical experience is said to be the absence of any distinction between subject and object. An immediacy this extreme has been found to be destructive of epistemic value. For either the knowing or believing subject has disappeared into the object, or, conversely, the object drops out of the picture, leaving us with a pure subjectivity. Even when mystical talk of an identification of subject and object is not taken so literally, there is often a tendency to treat the experience on the model of one's experience of one's own feelings; but this too proves subversive of the idea that one is thereby justified in any beliefs about something other than oneself.

Where else can we look for an established practice of more immediate theological statements? I believe that within normal Christian experience we find, in varying degrees, something called the sense of the presence of God. This may take many forms: a sense of being comforted by God while in distress; a sense of being guided by God in one's actions or words; a sense of the glory of God pervading the environment; a sense of being flooded with the love of God, with a consequent urge to act as a channel of this to the people around one; and so on. I believe that these cases are best pegged at the intermediate point of our scale. Like the case of perceptual judgments about physical objects, the standard learned procedure is to categorize what is happening in "objective" terms—in this case, in terms of God's presence, action, characteristics, etc. But in both cases, it does not take much reflection to recognize a layer of private experience, which one could describe in another language-game without theological (physical-object) commitments, *through* which one is experiencing God (physical objects), and which one could be thought of as "interpreting" in the talk of God (physical objects). Thus, insofar as there *is* an established practice of such immediate judgments, one has the same kind of "internal" immediate justification for "God is present with me in my distress" as for "That tree across the street is losing its leaves."

IV

If I were a more typical Sprachspielist, I could end the paper at this point. "This language-game is played." It comes equipped with its own distinctive criteria of justification, truth, reality, and so on. From within the game some statements are to be termed true and the objects putatively referred to therein real, since these statements meet the appropriate standards of that game. And from outside the game there are no relevant standards on the basis of which one can discuss the question of whether there *are* any such entities as are envisaged in the ontology of this game, or whether any of the statements made in this game are really *true*. If you play the game, you are committed to those standards and their application; if you don't, you are not. And that's all that can be said.

But, as I made explicit earlier, I don't buy all that. I do regard language-games as distinguished by (largely unformulated and perhaps largely unformulatable) criteria, or practices, of immediate application of terms on the basis of experience, and by distinctive and irreducible conceptual schemes. This provides a certain measure of conceptual and epistemic autonomy for a given language-game. It means that you cannot both accept (play) that game *and also* consistently hold that all its terms must be definable from outside or that all its judgments are *rational* only if supportable from outside. But I do not buy the verificationist idea that concepts of truth and reality are tied to epistemic standards of justification or rationality. Hence I see no reason to abandon the common-sense conviction that whether a belief (judgment, statement, assertion, proposition) is true or not is solely a matter of whether what it is about *is* as it is said to be in the assertion; and that the population and constitution of reality, apart from our thought and talk, is what it is regardless of what language-games we devise and play. From this realist standpoint it is not only possible but inevitable that one should ask, of a given language-game, whether its epistemic criteria are so designed as to give us truths, or at least so designed that if we conform to those criteria we are very likely to accept truths.*

And we are similarly driven to ask whether the entities envisaged in the ontology of a given language-game really exist, and whether the distinctive concepts of a given language-game apply to the sorts of entities to which they are applied in that game. I will sum up all these questions in the formula: "Is this language-game in touch with reality?" It is, no doubt, very difficult, or perhaps impossible, to arrive at a definitive resolution of such questions. However I do not see how, as philosophers, we can avoid confronting them and dealing with them as best we can.

---

*Note that if a common concept of truth applies to all language-games, the way is opened for assertions validated in one language-game to contradict assertions validated in another. Where this happens, it is clear that at least one of the games is off the mark, and the task of evaluating language-games takes on a special urgency.

At this point the radical Sprachspielist will, no doubt, ask "From within what language-game will you conduct this inquiry?" And whatever answer I give he will accuse me of begging the question, either for the prosecution or for the defense. Very briefly, what I would say in such a discussion is this: (1) Since language-games are only relatively autonomous, claims in one can conflict with claims in another, can support or weaken claims in another, and so on. Even Phillips recognizes this possibility and allows that we must not accept anything in religious discourse that we know to be false elsewhere. Hence we have the familiar contextualist point that by taking certain things (language-games) as not in question for purposes of a certain inquiry, we will have a basis for looking into other things. (2) There are, I believe, certain language-game neutral standards and criteria, e.g., consistency and parsimony, as well as more elusive criteria of adequacy of explanation, that, since neutral, can be used in the higher-level language-game of evaluating language-games.

Is the Christian language-game in touch with reality? It does differ from the other games to which we have been analogizing it in ways that arouse doubts about this. Let's enumerate these points of difference.

1. Not everyone plays. This point can be usefully divided into two parts. (*a*) Not everyone plays *any* religious language-game.* (*b*) There are a number of apparently incompatible religious language-games, so that not even all the religionists play the Christian language-game. By contrast, we all play the physical-world game, the human-person game, and so on. Or, rather, those very few who do not are put away and systematically ignored.

2. Closely related to this virtual unanimity is the fact that even those who play (or many of them) can imagine what it is like not to do so; they can envisage alternatives

---

*Tillich and others would dispute this. To discuss the issue we would have to go into the definition of 'religion', and there is no space for that here.

to the particular religious language-game they do in fact play, including the more radical alternative of no religious language-game at all. In fact many players of a given religious game are adult converts either from another religious language-game, or from spectator status (at most). Such people can hardly avoid realizing what an alternative would be like. Whereas we all acquire the physical-world and human-person games well before we arrive at the age of reflection, at which time we find them so thoroughly ingrained that we find it extremely difficult to envisage sitting them out, or to envisage what we would be playing instead. Even when very ingenious philosophers try to describe an alternative way of talking about what we perceive, it is usually unclear whether they have succeeded.

3. Even among the players there is a great deal of uncertainty about various moves, particularly the epistemically immediate applications of terms. It is not at all infrequent for believers to be uncertain as to whether God was speaking to them at a certain moment, as to whether a certain event was a revelation of God's will to them, as to whether God was really calling them to a certain vocation. It is almost as if, in our perceptual commerce with the physical world, we were always peering at objects through a dense fog. Indeterminacy also affects other aspects of the game. There is often puzzlement over how to understand talk about God. I do not mean philosophical puzzlement, which is obviously present to a high degree with respect to physical-object talk. I am thinking rather of puzzlement at the level of the practical use of the conceptual framework. Does it really make sense to address requests to God, since He will presumably do what is best, whatever we request? How can the New Life both be the work of the Holy Spirit within us and also our doing? We don't have the same sense of practical mastery in the wielding of these concepts that we have in familiar secular language-games.

Finally there is often indeterminacy as to whether one is within this sphere of practice. Do I really believe? Am I really committed to Christ?

4. Mastery of the Christian language-game is un-equally distributed among the participants. Clearly the capacity to make confident statements about God on the basis of experience varies widely from the saints to the all-but-nominal Christian. Even if we exclude from the roster those who are totally lacking in any capacity to discern God in experience, it still remains true that this capacity is only fitfully exercised by many Christians. A sense of the presence of God, much less an experience of God revealing His specific will for one, may come to a given person only in rare moments. At the other end of the spectrum we have the masters of the spiritual life, for whom God is a more or less constant part of their experienced environment. Hence authority plays a much larger role here than in our other language-games. Or, to put it another way, most participants get a much greater proportion of their information second-hand than is the case with physical objects. Of course, even with respect to the physical world, I would know far less than I do if I had to rely solely on my own experience. This is largely because of the limited spatio-temporal range of one person's perceptual experience, although in some cases I cannot appreciate what is right under my nose because of lack of expertise. Nevertheless, the point remains that where sense perception of physical objects is concerned, we are all equally experts with respect to a very large range of perceptibilia. Any normal human being can recognize a great range of familiar perceptible objects. Whereas in the Christian language-game many participants do not recognize God when He is intimately present, i.e., all the time. A favored few function as the primary recipients of divine revelation, and the experi-ence of the others functions primarily (as far as its cognitive function is concerned) as a partial confirmation

of the body of revealed truth at the core of the doctrinal
tradition.

5. There is another striking difference with at least the
physical-world language-game. Our confidence that we
are really on to something with physical-object talk is
shored up by the fact that the predictions we make within
the game are, by and large, borne out. Or at least, the
longer we play, the better position we are in to make
accurate predictions within the game. Our basic mastery
of the game puts us in a position to learn from experience
how various kinds of physical objects react to various
circumstances, which in turn puts us in a position to make
accurate predictions within the game. If we weren't, in
large measure, telling it like it is in this game, why should
our predictions pan out so often? There is nothing like
this in the Christian language-game. Learning to play the
game does *not* put us in a position to learn the conditions
under which God will speak to us (much less what He will
say when He does!), when He will shape the course of
events in one way rather than another, when He will
vouchsafe an unmistakable sense of His presence. Familiar sayings like "Blessed are the pure in heart, for they
shall see God," do not really hold up as reliable recipes.
Even the masters of the spiritual life explicitly disavow
any aspiration to discern any lawlike regularities in God's
activity (at least any lawlike regularities that we can
formulate), or to provide reliable rules for getting in
touch.

All together these differences add up to a rather
considerable case against the supposition that the Christian language-game puts us in touch with reality. The
attack can be usefully divided into two waves. The first,
an attack from without, depends on some very general
assumptions about what it takes to be in contact with
objective reality. The second, an insurrection from
within, bases itself on certain fundamental features of
God as depicted within the Christian language-game.

V

The first argument can be stated as follows: If Christianity did constitute a way of getting in touch with an objective reality, why shouldn't all normal adult beings learn to do so (at least all those who have been given the opportunity), as is the case with the other language-games we have been considering? And among those who do play the game, why is their mastery of it so often shaky, for the most part, and so unevenly distributed? Given these facts about the Christian language-game, isn't it more reasonable to suppose that the whole thing has some subjective origin? Isn't the unequal distribution and lack of mastery best explained by some such supposition as this? The "masters of the spiritual life" are persons whose constitution disposes them to certain kinds of abnormal states of mind. It is natural for them to interpret these experiences in terms of contact with a mysterious supreme reality. Then the bulk of the population, for whom religious belief satisfies basic psychological needs, tries, with only partial success, to convince themselves that they sometimes have experience of God as well, though some clear-headed individuals see through all this and opt out of the game.

So far as I can see, the religious form of life *can* be explained along these lines. But the argument that it *must* be explained this way, or even that this is the *best* explanation, is based on a highly questionable assumption, viz., if we are to have any cognitive access at all to X (if we are able to talk at all about X), we must have the sort of universal and (in practice) mostly unproblematic access we have to physical objects. In other words it takes an all-or-nothing approach to cognitive access. But, on the face of it, this is thoroughly unreasonable. It would seem to me *a priori* much more probable that different orders of reality are accessible to us in different degrees. Even within familiar modes of reality we find such differentiations. Middle-sized physical objects are more readily accessible, and less dubitable, than their fine structure. Inanimate nature is more clearly intelligible than personal agents. The structure of rocks reveals itself to us more clearly than the structure of language. And so on. Why shouldn't there be a reality that is elusive to our cognitive grasp in just the way God is in the Christian language-game?

In fact, there are reasons within the language-game to expect that elusiveness. Christianity and other theistic religions, in their most developed forms, stress the transcendence of God, His "wholly other-ness," our incapacity to capture Him in the sorts of concepts we find natural. Is it any surprise that our awareness and understanding of such a Being should be as fitful and uncertain as we actually find it in the Christian language-game?

This built-in cognitive elusiveness of God can also go some way toward explaining the multiplicity of religious language-games. If our natural powers are so little suited to grasping the nature and operations of God, it is the reverse of surprising that our attempts to do so should produce a variety of apparently incompatible formulations. That is what regularly happens in science when a phenomenon is not well understood, and our comprehension of God must be much weaker than, e.g., the understanding of heat or electricity in the eighteenth century.

Nor is the argument improved by focusing on the last difference mentioned above, that in the Christian language-game we do not succeed in discerning regularities that give us a basis for reliable prediction. It's true that this does give us a reason for imputing objectivity to the physical-world language-game that we lack in Christian discourse. But we certainly are not justified in supposing such success to be *necessary* for objectivity. Here again we can make a more general point, and one based on specific features of the language-game at hand. The more general point is that we should not suppose all types of reality to equally exhibit regularities discernible by us, and hence to behave in equally predictable ways. Quite apart from religion, we are much less able to predict human behavior than the operations of inanimate substances and forces. And it is well recognized that so long as we stick to phenomenal language and do not mix in considerations from the physical environment, we cannot find any regularities at all. (Sense impressions may be regularly connected with physical causes, but they are not regularly connected with each other.) And yet we do not take sense impressions or human persons to be the less objectively real for all that.

The more specific point again has to do with God's transcendence. If God is so different from anything in the natural world, it is not surprising that we should be unable to discern any predictive regularities in His "behavior." To make such discernment a necessary condition of objectivity is simply to refuse, *a priori*, to consider the possibility that such a Being exists.

VI

The attack from within can be stated as follows. "You Christians insist that God is benevolent, loving, merciful. You also hold that the highest good for man, man's ultimate end, is the knowledge and love of God. Surely, then, if such a God exists and is omnipotent, He would see to it that the knowledge of His existence, character, and purposes, are much more widely distributed and much more firmly held than is the case in your 'language-game' or in the totality of religious 'language-games'. Hence we can argue from fundamental principles of the Christian language-game that the differences listed earlier betoken a lack of existence of its object."

This is a powerful argument. In fact, it is just a particular form of the problem of evil—perhaps the most difficult form of that problem. For widespread ignor-

ance and rejection of God is, from the Christian point of
view, the greatest of evils. Why would an omnipotent,
loving God allow such an evil to mar His universe? I don't
pretend to have an adequate answer to this question, any
more than to other versions of the problem of evil that
focus on suffering or other evils. I am far from supposing that I can *see* that the way things are, in this and other
respects, is just the way that would be chosen by an
omnipotent and loving creator. Wouldn't it be presumptuous, indeed sinfully presumptuous, of me to suppose
that I can see the details of the divine plan? Nevertheless
something can be said. We can at least point to certain
important features of the Christian story about the
divine-human situation that help us to understand the
spottiness of our knowledge of God. This will not enable
us to understand just *why* a loving omnipotent deity
would set things up this way; but at least it indicates that
the troubling facts in question would not be contrary to
expectations, given certain basic features of the game.

The main point is this. It is fundamental to the Christian story that our awareness of God and understanding
of His nature and His will for us is not a purely cognitive
achievement. It requires the involvement of the whole
person; in Tillich's terms "faith" is a "centered" act of the
individual. Mastery of the Christian language-game (including mastery of the practice of immediate application
of theological terms) is not independent of the details of
the person's conative and affective life, in the way mastery of the physical-object language-game is.* God is

---

*Even here this independence may not be as great as traditionally supposed.
The researches of Freud and others have revealed to us the extent to which
normal cognitive development is dependent on a willingness to renounce the
immediately more gratifying "infantile omnipotence" and satisfaction in fantasy, in favor of the more demanding "reality principle," which involves
coming to terms with the world as presented in the physical-object and other
language-games. It has been convincingly shown that some disturbances in

always there; we don't have to travel to distant climes, much less to distant planets, to see Him and enjoy His presence. But He reveals Himself clearly, unmistakably, and in detail only to those who have responded to His call, have made a stable commitment to Him, have put Him at the center of their lives, and have opened themselves to His influence, His voice, His guidance. Now this is no trivial matter. To put oneself in this position, not just in a passing moment of enthusiasm, but for the rest of one's life, even in the periods when the going is rough, requires a more or less complete break with one's past life; it requires a stubborn resistance to a great variety of temptations to compromise, to take a vacation, to temporize, to take the whole thing as imaginary and so on. A sincere attempt to lead the Christian life makes things much more difficult in many ways. The fact that mastery of the language-game has these kinds of prerequisites throws some light, from inside the game, on the fact that mastery is not evenly distributed throughout the population, and that, indeed, secure mastery is reserved, in this life, for a very few who have devoted themselves to the spiritual life (not necessarily in isolation from the world) and have persisted in it. As previously noted, I do *not* claim that this consideration shows us *why* God would have set these prerequisites for mastery of this language-game. It only brings out the way in which some fundamental features of the divine-human situation as depicted in the Christian language-game render it understandable that it should have the kind of distribution it has.

---

cognitive development are due to inability or unwillingness to make this crucial transition. There is an obvious analogy with the Christian story as to what it takes to become securely stationed within the Christian language-game and to get in a position to recognize divine reality, an analogy that calls into question Freud's penchant for assimilating Christian belief to the earlier, infantile psychological attitudes.

VII

So far this critical section of the paper has been devoted to attempts to turn aside arguments against the objectivity of the Christian language-game. What positive reasons are there to regard it as objective? It will long since have been clear that I would not seek to answer this question by establishing reality of God from outside the Christian language-game, either by some overarching metaphysical scheme, or from within some other parochial language-game. For my money, we cannot establish the objectivity of any of the other language-games (including those of which we normally feel most secure, like the physical-world game) in either of these ways. What can we do to "defend," e.g., the physical-world language-game against its "cultured despisers"? So far as I can see, we can only (1) point to the fact (which itself cannot be established except, in part, by playing the game in question) that it is a going concern, an established practice, in which we participate. ("This language-game is played.") (2) We can determine whether it contradicts anything that is firmly established in other language-games we play. (3) We can see whether it is internally coherent. This involves such questions as: Do the entities within the range of this game behave and reveal themselves to our experience in ways that are not counterindicated by the categoreal nature of these entities? The physical-world game pretty clearly passes these tests.

Note that, for the most part, we cannot carry out these tests without using the language-game being tested. We cannot determine whether there *is* an established social practice of applying physical-object terms on the basis of experience without making observations on the speech and behavior of other persons in interaction with their environment; and this requires us to note the presence and the behavior of physical objects. Again, we cannot apply the third test without determining, from within the physical-world game, that physical objects *are* behaving in certain ways. Thus we can only test the game by using the game in the test, thereby presupposing that its ontology, etc., is valid. Does this make the test circular? At least it shows that the physical-world game can only be tested from within, that the crucial test is one of internal coherence. Do the detailed results obtainable within the game cohere with its basic assumptions?

I would suggest that the Christian language-game passes these tests too, when they are given appropriate interpretations. The need for "appropriate interpretation," i.e., appropriate to the language-game being tested, comes from the fact that these tests contain variables or "blanks" to be filled in differently for different language-games. Thus, e.g., the third test makes reference to the categoreal nature of the entities that make up the ontology of the language-game in question. As for (1), this language-game *is* played. Of course it is not played as widely or as stably or securely as the physical-world game; but, as we have been arguing, the nature of the subject matter (as revealed from within the game) makes it understandable that it should be played in this spotty fashion.* (2) The Christian language-game, in its more sophisticated versions, does not contradict anything that is firmly established in other games *we* play. (3) The behavior of God, as revealed in the Christian language-game, is in line, roughly speaking, with what one could reasonably expect from the categoreal features of God, as depicted within this language-game. Since this point is a rather complicated one, I had better

---

*This illustrates the point that even though test (1) looks as if it takes exactly the same form for all language-games ("Is the game played or not?"), in fact the standards for whether it is an "established practice" or a "going concern" will differ, depending on how the language-game represents its subject matter. If the physical-object language-game were played as spottily as the Christian language-game, then, given the way physical objects are represented in that game, that *would* be an indication that something is amiss.

elaborate it a bit, even though most of the pieces will be drawn from the previous exposition.

First, there is the point brought out earlier, that since God is not the sort of being whose activities we could reasonably expect to display any regularities discernible by us, the lack of predictive success is no mark against the language-game. But then in what way is the third test applicable? If the point is simply that since God is wholly other, anything goes, so far as we can see, that is, in effect, to declare the third test inapplicable. I don't see it quite that way, though I do believe that the "anything goes" attitude is a useful corrective to the "If God really exists the way He would have set things up is . . ." attitude. I believe the truth lies somewhere in between. As usual, our task in theology is to walk the tightrope between anthropomorphism, which evinces overweening pride, and agnosticism, which evinces the equally serious sin of despair. So, as I see it, it's like this. Christian theology does involve characterizing God—as creator, as omnipotent, as loving, as having a certain purpose for His creation, as laying down a pattern for human life. These characterizations give rise to various (rough, unspecific) expectations as to what we will find in the world. But this positive theology must be tempered in various ways: by the point that the positive predicates can be true of God only in a sense that is appropriate to God's categoreal nature; and by the point that we cannot aspire to understand the details of God's plans and their implementation. These qualifications have the effect of considerably softening the even very unspecific expectations we draw from the positive theology, thereby rendering infeasible any crucial experiments. As argued above, we cannot dismiss Christianity on the grounds that God has not revealed Himself in ways *we* would expect Him to if He exists as a loving, omnipotent Being. On the other hand, the expectations from the positive theology are not to be dismissed totally. If the Christian account is at least roughly correct, we would expect that one who turns to

God in the way called for and perseveres in the spiritual life will grow in that life and, in addition to the doubtlessly more important noncognitive aspects of that growth, will come to a clearer, more constant awareness of God and a securer grasp of His will and purposes, at least to the extent that they impinge on that person's practical concerns. This is the point that most needs to be added to the earlier rebuttal of the critic's case. The Christian life, or, in the present parlance, seriously playing the Christian language-game, is self-justifying and self-fulfilling. As we persist in it, we come to a fuller and more secure awareness of the reality and action of God, not in ways and under conditions that we could have anticipated in advance, but in ways that we come to see as right and proper as we advance in that life.* Indeed, I take it, this is what is most basically responsible for the fact that the game continues to be played almost two thousand years after its initiation. Whatever the social, economic, psychological, and other needs and functions that have played a role in the maintenance of the Christian church, I simply cannot believe that it would have

---

*It may well be charged that we have set things up so that there can be only positive evidence for the objectivity of the language-game; nothing is allowed to count as negative evidence. That charge cannot be sustained as stated, for clearly I do allow for the possibility of negative evidence, e.g., contradictions between beliefs within and without the language-game. But a more specific objection is that we have set things up so that facts about the occurrence of religious experiences are allowed to count only as positive evidence. About this I will say the following. (1) This is true. Since we cannot hope to anticipate the patterns of the divine operation, God's nonrevelation at any point cannot count as evidence against His existence, but whenever He does reveal Himself that is a mark in His favor. (2) But *I* didn't set it up this way. This "set-up" is deeply imbedded in the Christian (and other developed theistic) conception of God. Now if the features of that concept responsible for this asymmetry were developed in order to protect the scheme from disconfirmation, this would be highly suspicious. But, and this is the crucial point, the complex blend of positive and negative theology that we have in this language-game developed, I believe, from quite other roots. Hence the evidential asymmetry is a consequence of integral features of the language-game that were basically a response to other demands.

continued to play a major role in our culture unless the most dedicated practitioners had continued to find in its practice an ever-deepening realization of the presence and the action of God in our lives, and had not succeeded, to some extent, in communicating what they had discovered to players at lower stages of mastery. So perhaps in the end this point merges into the fact that "This language-game is played," once we appreciate what is presupposed by the latter.

There are many other matters which have not been touched on. (1) What implications does this approach have for the explication of theological concepts? If theological talk does indeed constitute an integral part of a total practice that essentially involves nonlinguistic aspects, how does that help us to understand what it is for God to forgive, speak, or love? (2) I would also like to explore, from this point of view, the *structure* of theological belief—how to distinguish between the more and the less fundamental commitments, and how to think of the latter as resting on the former. (3) Should we distinguish different Christian language-games corresponding to fundamental differences within the Christian tradition? (4) Is it possible, on this approach, for outsiders to understand Christian doctrine? And if not, how is conversion possible?

But I have been able only to give some sketchy idea of how one might try to construe Christian discourse as a "language-game" that enjoys a certain autonomy— ontologically, semantically, and epistemologically— without sacrificing traditional claims to objective truth.